# Successful Lace Knitting
## Celebrating the Work of Dorothy Reade

*Donna Druchunas*

*Martingale*®
& COMPANY

## Credits

President & CEO: Tom Wierzbicki

Editor in Chief: Mary V. Green

Managing Editor: Tina Cook

Developmental Editor: Karen Costello Soltys

Technical Editor: Ursula Reikes

Copy Editor: Melissa Bryan

Design Director: Stan Green

Production Manager: Regina Girard

Illustrators: Laurel Strand & Robin Strobel

Cover & Text Designer: Shelly Garrisson

Fashion Photographer: Brent Kane

Photo credits: Pages 6, 7, 8, 10, 11, 13, 16, 18, 20, 21, 23, and 24, photos by Arthur C. Reade; pages 7, 17, 23, and 25, photos by Dominic Cotignola; page 9, photo by defunct studio; pages 22 and 25, photo by the *Eugene Register-Guard*.

4492567+ 1/11

## Mission Statement
Dedicated to providing quality products and service to inspire creativity.

Successful Lace Knitting:
Celebrating the Work of Dorothy Reade

© 2010 by Donna Druchunas

Martingale & Company
20205 144th Ave. NE
Woodinville, WA 98072-8478 USA
www.martingale-pub.com

Printed in China
15 14 13 12 11 10      8 7 6 5 4 3 2 1

**Library of Congress Cataloging-in-Publication Data**
Library of Congress Control Number: 2010003686

ISBN: 978-1-56477-976-2

## Dedication

To Donna Reade Nixon, for her generosity and enthusiasm

## Acknowledgments

This book would not exist without the garments submitted by all of the wonderful designers and all of the excellent work done by the staff at Martingale & Company. Special thanks to Donna Reade Nixon for being so generous with her time and for sharing all of her mother's papers and work with me; to Alice Sherp for encouraging me to write this book, for letting me borrow and publish the pattern for Dorothy Reade's stole, and for various help and support along the way; and to Deb Robson for sharing her editing and knitting expertise. I can't thank you all enough!

# Contents

45

81

# Introduction

If you knit, chances are you've heard of Barbara Walker, Elizabeth Zimmermann, and Mary Walker Phillips. But you may not have heard of Dorothy Reade. Yet these ingenious women were all equally responsible for the rise of knitting's popularity in the United States in the latter half of the twentieth century. It's a mystery why Reade, whose creativity and output were second to none, is not as well known today as her compatriots. In addition to her independent work, she contributed patterns to Barbara Walker's stitch dictionaries, sparred with Elizabeth Zimmermann about knitting techniques, and created knitted art pieces that stand the test of time along with those by Mary Walker Phillips. Between 1964 and 1969 alone, Dorothy Reade's handspun, hand-knitted pieces were featured in almost 20 exhibits and museums. In addition, she taught knitting and spinning workshops and pioneered the use of charts for communicating complex knitting instructions.

I first heard of Dorothy Reade in 2004 when I was doing research for *Arctic Lace*, my book of knitted projects and stories inspired by Alaska's Native knitters. Digging through newspaper and magazine articles from the late 1960s, I found a photo of a 60-year-old woman at a spinning wheel. Her yarn was so fine that it looked like a spider's silk.

Dorothy Reade sometimes jokingly called herself a spider. Although she had learned to knit as a child, she'd been spinning for only a few years when the photo was taken. As a younger woman, she made baby blankets and sweaters for her daughter and as gifts for her friends. By the '60s, she was perfecting her skills and letting her creativity flow. Her favorite projects were fine lace shawls knitted with her handspun yarns.

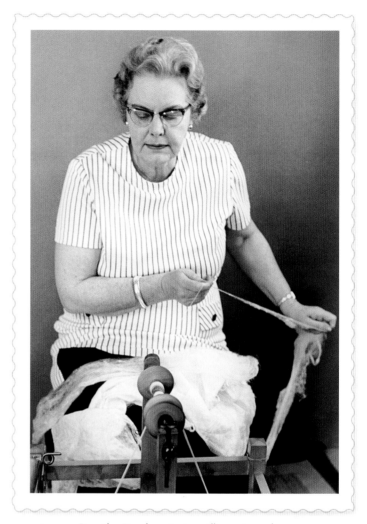

Dorothy Reade spinning silk waste on her Canadian Madewell wheel

Her superb spinning and knitting skills allowed Reade to teach workshops for the fledgling Oomingmak Knitting Co-op in Alaska, the subject of *Arctic Lace*. Although her work was only a small part of the Oomingmak story, I made a quick note to learn more about her.

In 2006, I was in Alaska to teach a workshop for the book launch of *Arctic Lace*. There I met Alice Scherp, who had known Dorothy Reade and still kept in touch with her daughter, Donna Reade Nixon. Alice told me, "[Dorothy Reade] was my teacher and friend and inspired my love of fine spinning and lace knitting." Before I knew it, I was sending an email to Donna, telling her that I wanted to learn more about her mother so I could write a book about her.

Dorothy Reade drew all her charts by hand on graph paper.

Dorothy Reade had a strong and energetic personality and style. With her daughter's generous permission, I have quoted Reade's own words extensively. I've had access to books, articles, and letters she wrote (published and in draft form), as well as interviews she gave during the 1950s, '60s, and '70s.

Donna Nixon displaying handspun, hand-knit lace shawl made by her mother

The projects on the following pages all incorporate original stitch patterns designed by Dorothy Reade and published in her book *25 Original Knitting Designs*. I wanted to showcase the patterns with the most original and unique projects possible, so I invited other designers to contribute ideas for this book. I sent each designer one of Dorothy Reade's charts and asked her to create something especially suited to that pattern stitch. The resulting projects are stunning and much more diverse than what would have appeared in these pages had I designed all of the projects myself.

# Who Was Dorothy Reade?

Almost 5,000 miles away from her Eugene, Oregon, home, in a small village outside of Lima, Peru, a gray-haired woman wearing cat-eye glasses and a pearl necklace was following a trail to hidden treasure. For Dorothy Reade, this trip was a delightful adventure. She attended a reception in the presidential palace, ate barbequed goat and sampled *chicha* (fermented maize drink) at a *pachamanca* (earth-pit barbeque), climbed the steps of the Temple of the Sun at Pachacamac, examined mummies' shrouds, watched Peruvian dancers in the pebbled courtyard of an old mansion, and visited artisans in street markets.

But it was in the Museo Oro del Peru—the Peruvian Gold Museum—that Reade found what she was searching for. She later wrote, "Here were assembled the glories of ancient Peru. Jewel studded weavings, jewel studded feather garments, masks, crowns, cups, ceremonial and funerary objects . . . the most exquisitely delicate necklaces and earrings." Yet Reade wasn't captivated by the sapphires, rubies, or gold. She was obsessed instead with the intricate textile handwork: the woven capes, handspun alpaca yarn, and chullos (knitted caps).

Dorothy Reade had journeyed to Peru for the General Assembly of the World Crafts Council. Although she spoke no Spanish or Quechua, she shared skills and enthusiasm across cultural barriers by using the language of hands.

Dorothy Reade at the 1968 General Assembly of the World Crafts Council in Lima, Peru

Knitted lace motifs inspired by Peruvian textiles, designed and knit by Dorothy Reade

Just months earlier, Reade was facing a blizzard at 30° below zero in Alaska, where she had been chasing down the "Golden Fleece of the Arctic"—another hidden treasure, the luxurious underdown of the musk ox. The shaggy, prehistoric-looking musk ox held a secret that has recently become well known to knitters, although it's still the stuff of legend. Beneath their long, coarse guard hairs, musk oxen grow fine, soft down—called *qiviut*—that makes cashmere seem commonplace by comparison. The indigenous peoples of Alaska, Canada, and Greenland stuffed the fiber into their winter boots. But spinning and knitting were not known to arctic needle workers before Europeans arrived. Although qiviut had been familiar to explorers and merchants since the late seventeenth century, it had never been used for textile production. When Reade experimented with the fiber in the 1960s, she accomplished something explorers and adventurers had failed to do: she discovered a way to create luxurious products made from qiviut and launch an Alaskan industry.

After corresponding with anthropologists and biologists at the University of Alaska at Fairbanks, and spending nine months experimenting with the unusual fiber, Dorothy Reade traveled north to meet the Native Alaskan women who would be the owners and artisans in the new adventure that became Oomingmak. There, in icy weather and without a common spoken language, Reade found a way to communicate about the fine points of knitting.

Like Indiana Jones and Lara Croft, Dorothy Reade traveled to exotic places to satisfy her curiosity, study antiquities, examine the contents of tombs, and explore museum archives. Although she had traveled widely with her husband for his job, only after his retirement did she cross the globe on her own adventures.

At home in Eugene, Oregon, Reade was the quintessential lady of her era. She wore gloves

Dorothy Reade, circa 1935

and silk stockings, always carried a hanky and a roll of butter rum Life Savers in her purse, and ran an orderly home. As a young woman in the 1920s and '30s, she had set aside her dream to be an archaeologist because "ladies didn't do that." Only late in life did she retrieve that dream.

Ella Dorothy Sorensen had always been a bit of a rebel. In her twenties, she broke five men's hearts when she broke off five engagements. Dorothy's mother threw up her hands, but Dorothy wasn't moved. "I'd look at them," Reade later told her daughter, Donna, "and think, 'Fifty years across the breakfast table, I just can't do it!'"

When she finally did marry, at 29, it was to a man with whom Dorothy would never lead a boring life. Arthur C. Reade's career with the Army Corps of Engineers took his family across the United States and to Europe. Dorothy was a wonderful military wife with the flexibility and resilience to make a home for her family wherever they went.

During the years traveling for Arthur's work, adventure became part of the Reades' lives. Photos show Dorothy working in a mining camp, feeding donkeys, and wearing men's clothes. But in "normal" society, she always wore a dress. Outwardly conservative, she stood always in at least two worlds, naturally embracing the spirit of women's lib in her quest for knowledge and understanding.

While he seemed like an old-fashioned husband and father (his daughter was six years old before she realized his name wasn't "Sir"), Arthur Reade supported his wife's intellectual and artistic endeavors. He helped with equipment, took photographs for her books and exhibits, and drove her wherever she needed to go. Dorothy Reade never did get a driver's license; she'd far sooner ride a mule.

Dorothy Reade was a lady, a wife, a mother, a craftswoman, and an adventurer. But most of all, she became something of what she had dreamed of as a young girl: a knitting archaeologist. Her explorations of knitting techniques around the world foreshadowed the ideas that became popular later in the twentieth century. The grandmother who spent many mornings on a porch with her spinning wheel also traveled the world in search of textile treasures.

Dorothy Reade at mining camp, circa 1938

## In Her Own Words

There are literally millions of knitters in the world. In fact, knitting is so universal people say "I knit" in much the same way as they say "I cook." Yet this handcraft, one of the oldest in man's history, is still a stepchild among the arts. It need not be.

There have been many breakthroughs in other crafts, weaving, pottery, glass, metals, etc., in which old methods have been refined and new ones evolved. Why knitting has lagged so far behind is a mystery. There are a few brave souls today who are trying valiantly to break through this barrier. I do not consider myself brave, just exasperated, which is why I have been struggling for years to find easier ways of attacking the problems that arise when one wants to do something other than knit and purl.

Thousands of hours of analyzing research have shown that one of the biggest drawbacks is fear of change. Why do we knit stitches in certain ways? Because, right or wrong, that is the way it has always been done. If by chance someone has found a better way, it has rarely been given out so that other knitters could benefit.

This closed corporation idea has persisted through history. During the . . . Middle Ages, when the Knitters' Guild was at its height, it was as specialized as the Weavers' or Goldsmiths', and its secrets as closely guarded. It was only during the other great period in knitting (early Victorian) that books finally began to appear with written instructions for patterns, the same system we use today with almost no changes. Our method today is no improvement on the careful instructions in those delightful old books.

## KNITTING IT MY WAY

Knitting was a thread that ran through Reade's entire life. As a little girl she learned to knit from her mother, and she continued knitting to the end of her life. From the thumbless mittens she made when she was five to the sweaters she designed for her daughter and the lace shawls she knit when she was older, every project was an adventure. She hated using patterns, preferring instead to work up designs from scratch. Her daughter remembers Dorothy pulling out the measuring tapes every time she began a sweater.

In a manuscript entitled *Another Look at Knitting*, written when she was in her sixties, Dorothy Reade voiced her complaints about the state of knitting.

Dorothy Reade would have been thrilled to see the recent changes in knitting, but in the 1960s it was still "your grandmother's knitting." Although hippies were crocheting halter tops and making belts and plant hangers from macramé, most women around America were knitting from the line-by-line instructions that filled popular pattern books. Charts were almost nonexistent in American knitting books, and schematics were also rare. Often there was no information about gauge! Yarn companies did not want knitters to substitute yarns, and provided only information about their brand—omitting even the yardage and weight of the skeins. Experimentation and creativity were not encouraged.

A lace wall hanging featuring Dorothy Reade's favorite pattern stitch, Peruvian cats

Many of today's English-language knitting books still provide instructions that assume the knitter will make an item exactly as shown, although modern books do provide information for yarn substitution and gauge. In contrast, European and Japanese knitting books usually assume that knitters can use detailed schematics and charts to make garments on their own, changing sizes as needed. What a different perspective!

Despite many advances in knitting instructions, knitters are still often frustrated by patterns. Dorothy Reade, like Elizabeth Zimmermann, wanted to free knitters from slavishly following instructions, but the two women worked toward this goal from opposite directions. While Zimmermann was formulating a percentage system to allow knitters to figure out how to make a sweater at any gauge or size, Reade was working on a way to convert complex stitch patterns from error-prone text into clear charts.

## In Her Own Words

Reade complained about people's tendency to do things the same old way because "that's how it's always been done." In *Another Look at Knitting*, she gave a favorite example:

There are certain rules that have evolved over the long centuries of knitting history which have remained unchanged, and for good reason. They are the absolute basics of all knitting. Only a few persist to this day which are incorrect, an example of which is the use of Sl 1, K1, psso. This is generally considered to be the opposite of K2tog. Actually, knit 2 together through the back loops is the opposite of K2tog. Sl 1, K1, psso produces this effect "ㅅ" [left-slanting stitch]. K2tog makes a stitch that looks like this "/" [right-slanting stitch] and K2tog/tbl gives this "\" [twisted left-slanting stitch].

## In Her Own Words

She continued the discussion to its logical conclusion:

If you are curious as to what the opposite of Sl 1, K1, psso really is, "K1 return it to the left hand needle, slip the 2nd stitch on the left hand needle over this knit stitch, and then return the knit stitch to the right hand needle"! This is what I mean by analyzing stitches.

Elizabeth Zimmermann also hated fiddly stitches, and preferred slip-slip-knit to slip one, knit one, pass slipped stitch over. Designer Joan Schrouder from Eugene, Oregon, remembers hearing the two knitters arguing about the "true" opposite of knit two together. She recalls, "I met [Dorothy Reade] several times while she was still alive, at least 20 years ago, and had some interesting conversations with her about knitting . . . and her rather stubborn attitude about knit two together in back being the equal to knit two together. She even tried to bait Elizabeth Zimmermann into a public argument about it, but Elizabeth, being the more diplomatic of the two, ended the discussion with an 'Isn't it wonderful that knitters can choose which they prefer?'"

Both Dorothy Reade and Elizabeth Zimmermann wanted to empower each of us to make our own choices about life, including the nitty-gritty details of knitting.

## KNITTING AS ART

Later in life, Dorothy Reade came to appreciate the artistic possibilities of her craft, as well as art in many other forms. In addition to knitting, embroidery, and other needlework, she enjoyed pottery, and even worked on a kick-wheel and made her own glazes; she was an accomplished pastel and watercolor artist; and she played the piano and had a lovely soprano voice. Yet in the end, she chose to dedicate much of her energy to knitting and spinning.

At the same time that Dorothy Reade was articulating knitting's stepchild status in the art world, Mary Walker Phillips was launching her well-known experiments with knitting as art. In the 1960s and

One of Dorothy Reade's handspun, hand-knit lace pieces on display in a museum exhibition

'70s, Phillips published *Creative Knitting: A New Art Form*; *Step-by-Step Knitting: A Complete Introduction to the Craft of Knitting*; and *Knitting Counterpanes: Traditional Coverlet Patterns for Contemporary Knitters*. Perhaps Dorothy Reade was inspired by these books, or perhaps Mary Walker Phillips was inspired by Dorothy Reade's work. We will probably never know. Yet it's clear that both Phillips and Reade were interested not only in reviving apparently dying traditions but also in promoting textiles as a medium of artistic expression.

Among Reade's papers, I found a draft entitled "Renaissance of the Handcrafts in the 20th Century." In it, she talks about her dreams for seeing knitting rebound in popularity, and about the need to recognize knitting—and other handicrafts—as art. (I haven't discovered whether this piece was published.)

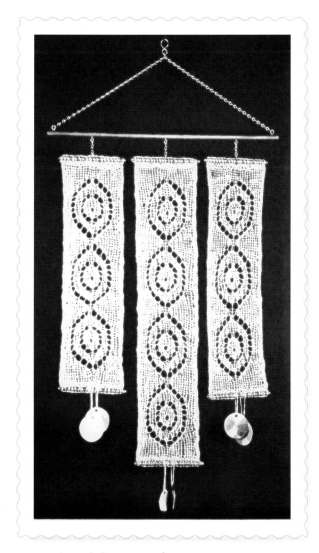

A wind chime, one of many unique pieces Dorothy Reade created using lace and knitting

In the middle of this century of science, automation, computers, and highly mercenary age, the recognition of the crafts is slowly emerging which is gratifying even if long overdue. It has also taken a long time to realize that the handcrafts must be regarded as part of the Arts. Actually there are three types of art.

Visual: painting, sculpture

Performing: stage, music, dance

Manual: The making of objects meant to be useful as well as ornamental. This includes pottery, weaving, metalwork, jewelry, enameling, glass, embroidery, as well as a host of related crafts, including, finally, knitting.

In all the arts, visual, performing and manual, there is one common denominator, the most primary of all tools, the hands. The use of the hands is especially essential in the handcrafts. They are the bridge of communication between an idea and a finished object.

Many people have the idea one has to be "artistic" to be creative, which is a lot of nonsense. Some of the worst examples of non-creativeness are put out by so-called artists, and many extraordinarily fine pieces are made by people who have never thought of themselves as artists. If you have made something, you have created something, whether it is your idea or someone else's. An original creation is one person's idea, but a creation can be the end product of many ideas from many people.

In education today, so much emphasis is placed on mental achievement there has been a tendency to downgrade manual skill, although an effort is now being made to bring this back as a very necessary part of the nation's economy.

**Her following thoughts could have been written today:**

I think one of the major causes of unrest, call it delinquency if you like, in the younger generation, and the overwhelming boredom among so many senior citizens is that many have never learned to create anything with their hands. Millions go through their entire life without ever having that sense of pure fulfillment which comes when you have made some actual piece, no matter what it might be. No machine made article could ever give the same pleasure to a child that his own string potholder, no matter how grubby, would. It all boils down to the fact that there are too many idle hands.

The beauty of this business of crafts is that there is no stopping point—ever. For instance in my own case, I have knit longer than I care to remember, and enjoyed it, but when I started working with the fibers themselves, the results were so surprising I needed to know more. This led me to experiment with all sorts of things, which of course included the knitting.

I found there are still many unexplored avenues even in crafts as old as spinning and knitting. The challenges I have been given at various times have been the most rewarding. Some of them I will probably never repeat, but the knowledge gained could be applied to other things.

## DOROTHY READE'S BOOKS

Dorothy Reade wrote four knitting books and published three of them. Each book focused on helping knitters find new and easier ways to approach their craft. Knitting from charts is central to all.

### 25 Original Knitting Designs

In June 1966, Dorothy Reade was excited. She wrote letters to friends and business associates telling them about her wonderful experiences visiting New York. While meeting with curators at the Cooper Union Museum, a branch of the Smithsonian where one of her knitted lace pieces was being exhibited, she had been introduced to an editor from Reinhold Publishing. The editor was excited about her inventive charting system. She wrote, "[T]he visit with Mr. K—— . . . really put the cap on everything. He never said one word about accepting the book, but plunged immediately into such things as format, layout, price, size, illustrations, possible publishing date and he would check with the publisher as to royalties and contract!! I left that office slightly punch-drunk and was still in a daze when I got on the plane. Having never come in contact with a publisher before, I have no idea if this is the usual procedure. In any case I hope he meant business."

On the strength of the meeting, she apparently broke off negotiations with another publisher. In a letter to that unidentified house, Reade wrote, "I regret causing you inconvenience, but after a most astonishing interview at Reinhold I somehow felt that the time was not yet for publication of bits and pieces which might cause confusion later on."

Things didn't go as smoothly as she hoped.

After fighting with two publishers who "wouldn't do it my way," as she told a reporter later, Reade published *25 Original Knitting Designs* herself in 1968. The details of her disagreements with publishers are lost, but fortunately for knitters everywhere, copies of her writings have survived.

写真は手編機を前に手芸を楽しむリード夫人

In 1966, Dorothy Reade made news in Japan for visiting the Japan Silk Association to research how best to blend silk and qiviut.

In *25 Original Knitting Designs*, Reade included her favorite techniques along with a collection of lace pattern stitches, all illustrated with her brand-new charting system. For $4.50, a bargain even then, a knitter received the original patterns, a how-to guide on knitting lace, and tips on incorporating the patterns into a variety of projects from place mats to sweaters.

The original pattern stitches—presented in this book with permission—range from simple diamonds and lozenges to ornate floral and lattice patterns. Reade's favorite pattern, a cat inspired by a Peruvian weaving, appears on the cover of her 1968 book and is used within several projects in this volume.

This cat design is a wonderful example of Reade's work in adapting designs from other types of artwork, from cultural artifacts, and from nature. The practice has since become common in the knitting world; motifs from international arts and crafts designs and from natural phenomena adapted into color, textured, and lace knitting have become widespread.

"I have resolutely refused to write these patterns down in the usual confused and error-prone method which has been in use for over a century," Reade wrote in the foreword. "Substitution of charts and symbols eliminates the ambiguity, confusion, errors, and many hours of work."

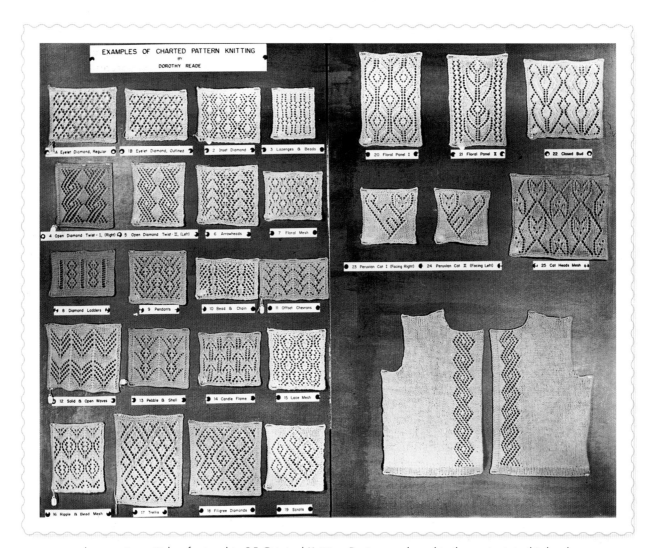

Lace pattern stitches featured in *25 Original Knitting Designs* and used in the projects in this book

The designs shown here in *Successful Lace Knitting* incorporate Dorothy Reade's timeless stitch patterns from *25 Original Knitting Designs*. As Reade would have wanted, the patterns are presented in chart form. Because charting conventions have evolved since Reade presented her ideas, I have created charts using modern symbols (see page 30).

## A Jacket Sweater with an Aran Accent

Aran knitting seemed to come second only to lace knitting in Reade's preferences. Among her papers I was thrilled to uncover an original copy of Heinz Edgar Kiewe's *Origin of the 'Isle of Aran' Knitting Designs*. This legendary paper is the source of many stories—and myths—about the intricate knitting done in the Aran Islands of Ireland. Buried in a pile of Reade's hand-drawn knitting charts, swatches, and photographs of knitting projects, I also found a photocopy of a pattern for an Aran sweater-and-accessory ensemble from a 1956 issue of *Woman's Day* magazine. The unnamed designer, presenting techniques unfamiliar to North American knitters of the time, suggested the use of toothpicks to work the cable crossings. Aran knitting caught on, and by the time my own grandmother was feverishly knitting "Irish Pattern" sweaters in the 1960s and '70s, cable needles had become readily available.

In 1969, Dorothy Reade published an Aran pattern booklet called *A Jacket Sweater with an Aran Accent*. She used it to teach workshops at Broadway department store in Eugene. The booklet includes a jacket pattern and 10 original Aran cable patterns, all charted—of course!—with her symbols.

Just as her charts simplified stitch instructions, Reade's sweater pattern simplified garment instructions. Instead of writing out many dense paragraphs of text, Reade laid out the entire pattern in a table on a single page. The table contained step-by-step instructions in a numbered list in the left column. Columns to the right clearly listed numbers for each size. A second page included a schematic drawing with numbers corresponding to the steps in

the instructions. Any of the 10 charted cable stitches could be used in the cardigan fronts, and knitters were expected to be able to add cable accents on their own. Dorothy Reade worked constantly to free knitters from rigid adherence to patterns.

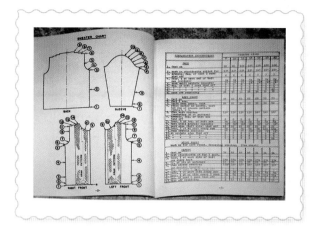

Dorothy Reade created a unique format for presenting knitting patterns.

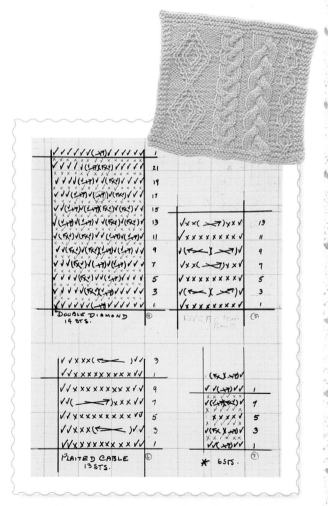

In addition to symbols for lace charts, Dorothy Reade also created a system for charting cables.

## Shorthand Knitting

In Dorothy Reade's third and final published booklet, *Shorthand Knitting: Decorative Panel Designs* (1970), she expanded on her use of charts and included 10 more pattern stitches, along with ideas for how to use them. The booklet includes basic patterns for using the stitches on scarves, stoles, place mats, afghans, sweaters, dresses, and even a wind chime! Reade's standard instructions for knitting from charts are also included.

Fanfare over Reade's revolutionary charting system had been growing, even years before publication of *Shorthand Knitting*. A headline in the July 31, 1968, edition of the *Eugene Register-Guard* proclaimed, "Eugenean Pushes Ancient Handicraft into the Jet Age."

As Thora Qaddumi, the women's editor, continued, "Would-be knitters who can't get past 'knit one, purl one' are offered hope through a new—even revolutionary—method of knitting developed by Mrs. Arthur C. Reade. Instead of the usual hieroglyphics, the rows of abbreviated instructions that often confuse even the most experienced knitters, Mrs. Reade offers a simple chart."

The jet-age comparison came from Reade herself. "We've been using horse and buggy methods in knitting in the jet age," she told the reporter. "Development of knitting methods came to a screeching halt in the 1840s."

Reade was approached by industrial designer Henry Dreyfuss about including her knitting symbols in a World Data Bank of symbology, which included traffic symbols, danger signs, and postal icons, in an attempt to create a worldwide graphical language. The experiment did not completely succeed—while symbols are used more widely today than they were in the past, there is still no universal symbol language. But the use of charts to simplify the communication of complicated knitting instructions continues to this day.

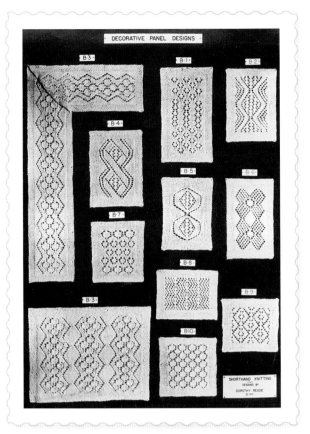

*Shorthand Knitting* does not include photographs; however, in Dorothy Reade's papers, I discovered a photo of the stitches charted in the book.

## Knitting Symbols and How to Use Them

Dorothy Reade's last, unpublished book continued her work with knitting symbols (see "Basic Symbols" on page 30) and also covered many other interesting knitting topics. Dorothy wanted to revive the craft of knitting by continuing to promote charted patterns. Her first book was intended to be "an appetizer," as she planned to write a "complete text on knitting." This larger book was never completed. Fortunately, a partial manuscript survives.

Although some of Reade's thoughts have been updated through further research, her early delving into the history of knitting was both prescient and inspiring.

## In Her Own Words

Knitting has a long, long history, going back thousands of years. Perhaps even some caveman tried it with a pair of sticks and a strand of some vine. It certainly is one of the oldest crafts.

One would think that by now we would be super-experts, but now, we seem to know less about it than they did 300 years ago. Certainly now-a-days one doesn't find beautiful tapestries, rugs, silk shirts and stockings, and delicate laces.

During the Middle Ages, when knitting was a recognized craft . . . It took about six years for an apprentice to become a Guild member, and then to graduate, as one might put it, he was required to create a special piece, perhaps a tapestry or a rug, much as a college graduate writes a thesis. . . . A few of these masterpieces survive . . . and the exquisite workmanship is enough to turn the modern knitter pale.

Most instructions were probably by word of mouth, but a good many must have been written down, quite possibly in some form of shorthand, and also charted. No doubt many facts and bits of information lie buried in museums, libraries, etc., but unless one knew exactly where to look, it would be very difficult to dig them out for ourselves, to say nothing of the time it would take.

The idea of actually writing down instructions and publishing them for knitters to work from does not appear to have started until the early 1800's. Except for the fact that they take a bit of translating into modern language, it is really easier to follow them than those in use today. Let's face it, instructions for knitting patterns today are cumbersome, archaic, frustrating, and downright exasperating!

Let us remind ourselves that we are every bit as smart as they were in the Middle Ages, but we just do not have the time to spend in serving a six year apprenticeship before we can take off on our own. So let us be modern. After all, when so many problems are solved by scientific methods—and Univac—why not do our own computing, and reduce all these complicated knitting terms to the lowest common denominator, a SYMBOL?

A number of knitting books (generally English and European) have included some information on symbols and charts, but for the average knitter they sometimes seem so involved that it is simpler to go back to the written direction.

I have long felt that a set of symbols which could be read and written down with ease and speed, and that would apply to any type of knitted pattern stitch (lace, Shetland, Aran Island, etc.) would be of considerable use, not only to experts but knitters as a whole.

# Dorothy Reade's Lace Knitting

Like many knitters today, Dorothy Reade was always looking for an exciting new challenge. When she discovered lace knitting, she fell in love forever. Her passion for lace led her to visit other countries for her research. She explored lace knitting traditions that were on the verge of dying out but have since become popular, and she developed her own unique system of lace knitting that launched the independence of Alaska's Oomingmak craftworkers.

## INSPIRATION

Reade's fine lacework was inspired by Shetland and Orenburg lace knitting, and she re-created shawls inspired by both traditions. When she learned how to spin, she found that she was fascinated by the possibilities offered through spinning fine yarns, which even further increased her interest in knitting lace. Her one-mile-per-ounce handspun merino yarn, which she knitted up into a mantilla,

or wedding veil, was used to argue for the removal of an Australian export ban that was keeping the breed of sheep out of the United States. The finished piece weighed just five-eighths of an ounce.

## Shetland

In 1964, Dorothy Reade was perhaps the only person in the United States knitting Shetland shawls, and the sole remaining knitters in Scotland were eight women, all over the age of 80, on the Isle of Unst.

Shetland lace was developed as a commercial product in the early 1940s, when hand knitting began to decline as sock-knitting machines came into use. Two people in particular were influential in spreading the popularity of these featherweight shawls. One was Edward Standed, an Oxford wholesaler who visited Shetland in 1839 and

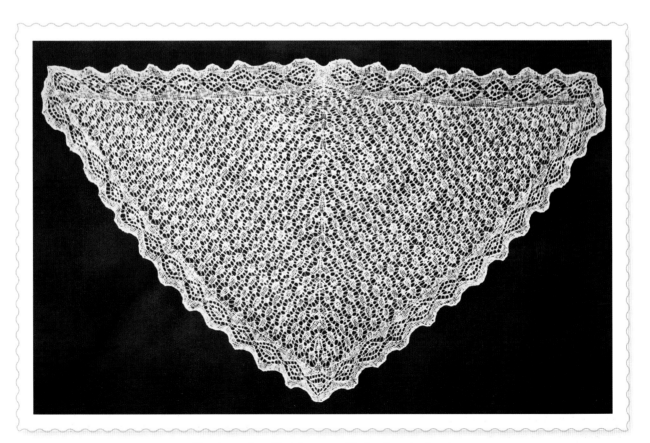

Handspun, hand-knit lace mantilla by Dorothy Reade

created an external market for the openwork shawls and hankies. The other was a 19-year-old widow named Margaret Currie. Margaret purchased a lace shawl from a woman in the marketplace and sent it to a friend, who showed the shawl to Queen Victoria's ladies in waiting. The garments caught on with society ladies throughout Europe. Eventually, machine-made lace overshadowed the hand-knitting industry. Although the industry will never be what it was, the Unst women began teaching spinning and knitting and, as a result, a few knitters are still employed in Shetland today.

Even though Shetland knitters were renowned for their speed, one Shetland shawl could take an entire year to make. Dorothy Reade could complete a shawl in five months, most likely because she had access to modern conveniences and did not have an outside job or a house full of young children.

## Orenburg

When Dorothy Reade received a gift of a moth-eaten Orenburg lace shawl that had been knitted around 1850 or 1860, she began trying to figure out how to make one. At the time, no information on this type of lace knitting was available in the United States.

Just as in Shetland, in Orenburg, Russia, two people were primarily responsible for the popularity of the lace shawls. Peter Ritchkov, a local historian and scientist who came to Orenburg in 1735, and his wife, Elena, promoted the idea of a cottage industry. By 1800, shawl knitting had become the region's most popular handcraft.

In the twentieth century, one tattered Orenburg shawl made its way into Dorothy Reade's hands. She carefully charted its pattern stitches with pencil on graph paper, spun yarn to match the antique, and knitted a reproduction. As usual, she couldn't resist her own creativity and she made some minor changes to the patterning.

Antique Orenburg lace shawl

Dorothy Reade was so inspired
by the antique Orenburg shawl that she recharted
the pattern stitches and knitted her own.

Dorothy Reade showing off her
delicate lace work for a newspaper article

## INNOVATIONS

Dorothy Reade was passionate about innovation and creativity. According to Kathy Sparks in *Song of the Muskox*, in 1965 Reade wrote, "I have spent some time with several knitting authors . . . and ended up a nervous wreck trying to keep my cool at the traditional hidebound attitudes still prevalent, which have been the stranglehold on new concepts."

### A Cottage Industry in Alaska

In the early 1960s, at the University of Alaska, Fairbanks, anthropologist John Teal was looking for a way to use qiviut to build a cottage industry in Alaska, similar to the projects that had flourished in Shetland and Orenburg. At the same time, Dorothy Reade was looking for new fibers with which to experiment. It took a while before their paths intersected, with good and long-lasting results.

Reade was asked to experiment with the fiber and report back to the university with her recommendations on its commercial use. After removing the guard hairs with tweezers, Reade spun several yarns (including blends with wool, silk, and Dacron) and then knitted sample garments. Using her talents at converting designs from different sources into knitting, she designed a lace pattern based on the carvings on a 1200-year-old ivory harpoon head found in the village of Mekoryuk.

Dorothy Reade's charting system was perfectly suited to the needs of the new knitters of Oomingmak, the Musk Ox Producers' Co-operative. Although many members were already expert knitters, they spoke Yup'ik or Inupiat and wouldn't have been able to follow English instructions. Today, 250 Native Alaskan women knit lace using Reade's techniques.

### Unique Stitch Designs

Even when she was knitting traditional-style garments, Dorothy Reade preferred to make things up as she went along. "It's no fun to copy," she told a reporter in 1964. "I usually start with the old pattern and make up my own pattern as I knit. Because I let my imagination run riot when I take up my knitting needles, I never know how the shawl will look. No two pieces I knit are ever alike."

Reade was especially proud of her work interpreting designs from antique lace and tapestries, mummies' shrouds, and Inuit ivory carvings. She wrote, "It is unfortunate that I seem to be the only one in the country able to convert from one medium to another, i.e. taking wood or stone carvings, weaving, painting, etc. and putting out workable knitting instruction." She would have loved many of the books that have been published recently, showing how contemporary designers have opened up new worlds of creativity and style by adapting ideas from Viking carvings, Celtic knot-work, African basketry and weaving, and pre-Columbian Andean textiles.

Dorothy Reade also designed stitch patterns purely from imagination. She used her stitches in her own creations, published some in her books, and contributed others to Barbara Walker's stitch treasuries.

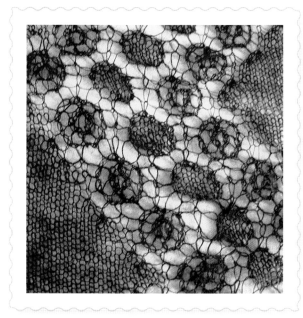

Some of Dorothy Reade's favorite designs used circular and curved lace motifs, a technique she felt was, unfortunately, "almost nonexistent and of which the knitting public seems to be unaware."

## Charts

Dorothy Reade may have been the first charting evangelist in America. She refused to write line-by-line instructions for her patterns. She thought charts were the Rosetta stone of knitting. She considered written instructions to be as indecipherable as hieroglyphics, requiring translation from a nonvisual language to a visual one. Based, perhaps, on charts she'd seen in Japanese or European knitting books, as well as the few that were used in American publications, Reade developed the charting system that she referred to as "shorthand knitting." With these symbols, she was able to teach Native Alaskan women—few of whom spoke English at the time—to knit delicate lace.

Dorothy Reade at her typewriter

As a reporter wrote, "Each symbol is a pictograph of a finished stitch. Those who knit recognize at once that a slash mark pictures the result of 'knit two together'." That was Dorothy Reade's goal: a system where each symbol looked like the resulting stitch so that knitters would be able to knit by looking at the picture and at their knitting. As she said, "When you get something simple enough, you get beginners interested."

In her first book, she wrote:

I found that most combinations could be reduced to a simple sign that showed what the stitch would look like. For instance, Sl 1, K2tog, psso, which completed looks like an inverted V. The symbol therefore became ∧. A yarn over results in a hole in the fabric so O suggested itself. . . . I found that about 75% of pattern designs could be boiled down to a very few symbols, which, when put on graph paper . . . created a picture of the resulting design.

The concept of using charts in knitting is not new. Many variations of symbols have appeared, but have not been adopted as a common practice, perhaps because many are so complicated that it takes longer to find out what they mean than it does to follow the written direction. To me, the whole idea of using symbols is a knitting shorthand that can be read and written quickly and easily.

Reade explained this to a reporter in 1973. "Having been a knitter for fifty years," she said, "I set out developing a new revolutionary method. Instead of the usual . . . rows of abbreviated instructions that baffle even an experienced knitter, I made up eight simple symbols that make knitting so easy even a 10-year-old can learn quickly."

## Spinning

Dorothy Reade learned to knit when she was five years old; she learned to spin at age 51. She considered spinning to be "an added impetus" to her lifelong interest in knitting. Once Reade learned to spin lace-weight yarns with merino, alpaca, and qiviut, her work exploded into the limelight.

Dorothy Reade spinning a fine, lace-weight yarn

Although she could spin a mile, or 1760 yards, of yarn from a single ounce of fiber, Reade found that a half mile per ounce was "more practical" for knitting shawls. (Reade's "half-mile" yarns measured 880 yards per ounce; today's commercial lace-weight yarns range from 200 to 400 yards per ounce.) Her yarns were so fine that she could fit 500 stitches on a 10-inch straight knitting needle. Her finest yarns were only 5/1000ths of an inch in diameter. A commercial yarn that thin would literally be a thread, but Reade's yarns retained a handspun yarn's loft and bounce, giving them a light texture and enough body for successful knitting yarns.

The curator of textiles at the Metropolitan Art Museum in New York heard about Reade's yarns and commissioned her to spin linen to repair a piece of sixteenth-century Italian lace. "It took me almost a month to spin one ounce," Reade wrote in an unpublished manuscript, "which ended in a mile of thread, two miles of exasperation, and, as this type of linen is spun wet, a set of corrugated fingertips." The finished thread, spun from Oregon flax, was a perfect match for the 300-year-old treasure.

Reade didn't limit herself to spinning luxury fibers. She also worked with more mundane materials, such as cotton, wool, nylon, Dacron, and silk waste, along with many blends. Although today many of these fibers are well known to knitters and spinners, in the 1960s and '70s they were unheard of. When Reade was told "nobody spins merino," she had to try. "Why I've even spun the lint from my dryer," she told a reporter in 1973. "But I have drawn the line at dog hair—setter hair spins beautifully, but the minute it's washed or worked it sticks out and can give you hives." She apparently never had the opportunity to spin Samoyed.

Dorothy Reade carding wool

# Lace Knitting Techniques

Dorothy Reade believed even beginning knitters could knit lace if they learned the basic stitches and worked from charts. I tried to learn how to knit lace several times before I found Reade's instructions and tips.

If I had only discovered these techniques earlier, I would have saved myself so much frustration. If I can learn to knit lace from Dorothy Reade's instructions, I know you can, too! The following pages include Reade's lace knitting instructions taken directly from *25 Original Knitting Patterns*, with fresh illustrations plus tip boxes and sidebars containing notes from my experience.

Dorothy Reade studied nineteenth-century knitting books and translated old lace stitch patterns into charts, but she never published her work in this area.

## LACE KNITTING BASICS FROM *25 Original Knitting Designs* by Dorothy Reade

This monograph is an answer to the many knitters who for years have requested publication of my designs. (I say "my designs" insofar as they have all been worked from scratch, and intensive research has shown no duplication.)

I have resolutely refused to write these patterns down in the usual confused and error-prone method which has been in use for over a century. Substitution of charts and symbols eliminates ambiguity, confusion, errors, and many hours of work. This small book employs the most frequently used symbols from my complete basic list.

While these designs were created for lace knitting in very fine yarn, they are versatile enough to be used in many ways with any type of yarn or needles. Each pattern can be used as a single panel; however many of the photographed samples have the repeat sections worked several times each way so that the over-all design is apparent, with the stitches contained in the chart itself outlined in black.

A few suggestions for using these designs are:

- Knitting yarn, single panel patterns; borders on sweaters, accents on dresses or shell blouses, edgings, afghan panels, etc.

- Knitting yarn, all over patterns; sweaters, blouses, dresses, blankets, afghans, pillows, etc.

- Linen or cotton; dresses, place mats (for table, TV trays, etc.), tablecloths, curtains, room dividers, hangings, etc.

- Very fine yarn and thread (weaving supply shops are your best bet for these); lace stoles, scarves, mantillas, mats, tablecloths.

The following illustrations give some examples of how designs can be incorporated.

## BASIC STITCHES IN LACE KNITTING

The designs in this book can be worked by the beginner as well as the advanced knitter if the basic stitches are mastered. For this reason, pictured explanations of these stitches are given so that their functions may be reviewed. While there are other variations of some of the principles, they are not used in the particular designs given in Dorothy Reade's original book. The symbols included in the directions are explained on page 30.

### Knit one (K)

Needle is inserted through the front of the stitch with the yarn being held at back.

### Knit one through the back loop (K1-tbl)

Needle is inserted from right to left through the loop at the back of the needle.

## Knit two together (K2tog)

Needle is inserted left to right through front of two stitches and knit together. Decrease of 1 stitch.

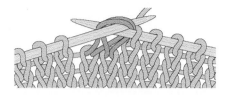

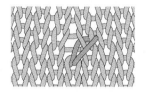

## Knit two together through the back loops (K2tog-tbl)

Insert needle from right to left through the back loops of two stitches and knit together. Decrease of one stitch.

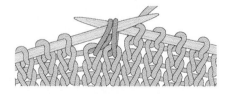

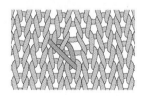

*A Note from Donna*

### LEFT-SLANTING DECREASES

Knit 2 together forms a right-slanting decrease, but there are several ways to make a decrease that slants to the left (see the illustration at bottom left).

Slip one knitwise, knit one, pass slipped stitch over (sl1-K1-psso)—This traditional decrease can be confusing because it requires three motions to make one stitch, disrupting the rhythm of the knitting and making it difficult to follow charts which show one square for each completed stitch.

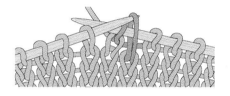

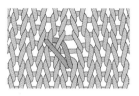

Slip, slip, knit (ssk)—Although this is faster and easier than sl1-K1-psso, it still requires three motions to complete one stitch.

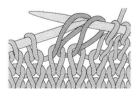

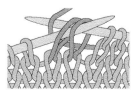

Knit two stitches together through the back loops (K2tog tbl)—Here, with Reade's favorite left-slanting decrease, we finally have a decrease that uses one motion to create one stitch. The chart symbol slants to the left, the stitch itself slants to the left, and when you insert the needle into the two stitches to knit them together through the back loops, the tip of the needle also points to the left. Knitting through the back loop, however, twists the finished stitch, so in thicker yarns, smoother yarns, and lighter-colored yarns, this stitch may not look exactly like a mirror image of knit two together. When working with fine lace-weight yarns, as Dorothy Reade most often did, the difference is not obvious.

## Slip one (Sl 1)

Slip needle into stitch as if to purl and transfer from one needle to the other without knitting.

## Slip one, knit two together, pass the slipped stitch over (Sl 1, k2tog, psso)

Slip one stitch from left to right needle, knit two stitches together, insert the left needle through slip stitch on right needle and pull it over the stitch formed by the knit two together. Decrease of two stitches.

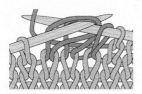 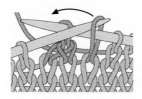

### A Note from Donna

## DOUBLE DECREASES

Double decreases begin with three stitches and end with one. Double decreases can also slant to the left or the right, or they can be vertical in orientation as well. The contributors to this book used several different double decreases in their designs.

Knit three stitches together (K3tog)—This is a right-slanting decrease.

Slip one stitch knitwise, knit two together, pass slipped stitch over (sl1-K2tog-psso)— This is a left-slanting double decrease. See illustration bottom left.

Slip two stitches knitwise, knit one, pass two slipped stitches over (sl2-K1-p2sso)—This is a center double decrease or a vertical double decrease.

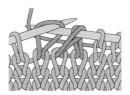 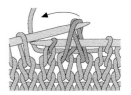

Slip two stitches together as if to knit. Knit the next stitch on the left needle.

Pass the two slipped stitches over the knit stitch on the right needle.

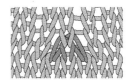

## Purl one (P)

Needle is inserted right to left through the front of the stitch, with yarn held at front.

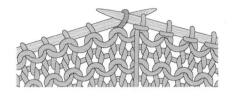

## Over (O) [now called yarn over (YO)]

Bring the yarn to the front *between* the needles before knitting next stitch.

Coming back on the purl side, work as regular purl stitch.

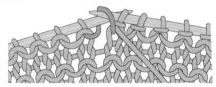

## Double overs (O, O) [now called yarn over twice (YO 2x)]

Bring yarn to front between needles, then over and to the front again. (Right around needle.)

When coming back on the purl side, purl one in the first of the two loops, then knit one in the second loop.

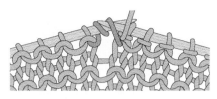

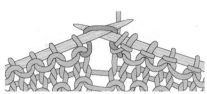

## Increase one stitch (Inc)

Only one method is used in this book. Knit one through the front, then knit one through the back of the *same* stitch.

---

*A Note from Donna*

### OTHER INCREASES USED IN SUCCESSFUL LACE KNITTING

The contributors to this book have used different increases in some of the projects: lifted left increase (LLinc), lifted right increase (LRinc), and make one (M1). See "Abbreviations" on page 108 for any unfamiliar terms in the instructions.

---

## POINTS OF EMPHASIS

These designs contain two specific departures from the usual method of knitting. As far as I have been able to ascertain, neither one has ever been brought to the attention of the knitting public, but they make the difference between ordinary workmanship and the professional touch.

1. The use of "knit two together through the back of the loops" (K2 tog. tbl). You will find a complete absence in this book of the usual "Sl 1, K1, psso." K2 tog. tbl is substituted at all times as the correct opposite of "knit two together" (K2 tog).

2. Outlining. This is to ensure clean smooth edges in the design. The stitch formed by purling an [yarn] "Over" is knit through the back of the loop (K1 tbl) in the following knit row. This principle will become very apparent when you come to study the charts. "K1 tbl" is also used as an accent stitch.

Two more small points that will make your knitting easier are:

1. Mark one of your needles in some manner; with a rubber band, a piece of colored Scotch tape, even a dab of bright nail polish, then use this marked needle for knitting your front [right side] rows. In this way, you can always be sure which side you are working on which is especially helpful when using dark yarn or knitting a reversible fabric.

2. Markers. The use of a loop marker to divide each repeat section in the more difficult designs will help you keep track of where you are. To make one of the markers, take a piece of thin yarn (different color from what you are working with) about 4 or 5 inches long, and tie it firmly around the needle. This will give two little tails hanging down which are excellent warning signals for the next repeat coming up. (It is of course slipped from one needle to the other, never knitted.) If the marker should land in the middle of a group of stitches to be worked (say Sl 1, K2 tog. psso) remove marker from needle, complete your stitch, then replace marker before going on. These loop markers are really easier to use than the plastic ones, as they do not fall off the needle or catch in the material.

## BASIC SYMBOLS

Possibly 50% of all knitting patterns in use today can be charted using only the few symbols shown below. Notice how the slanted symbols show the direction of the completed stitch.

### Symbol Systems

| | Dorothy Reade's | | This book's | |
|---|---|---|---|---|
| K on RS | X | | ☐ | K on RS, P on WS |
| P on WS | ☐ | | | |
| P on RS | ✓ | | • | P on RS, K on WS |
| K1 tbl | B | | ℺ | K1 tbl |
| YO | ● | | o | YO |
| sl 1-K2tog-psso | ⋀ | | ⋀ | sl 1-K2tog-psso |
| K2tog | / | | / | K2tog |
| K2tog tbl | \ | | \ | K2tog tbl or ssk |
| M1 | 1 | | M | M1 |

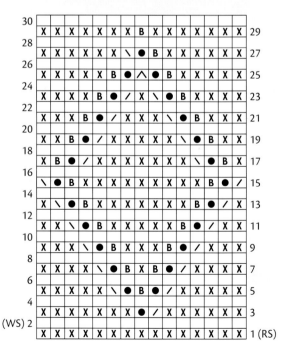

| 30 | X | X | X | X | X | X | X | B | X | X | X | X | X | X | X | 29 |
|---|---|---|---|---|---|---|---|---|---|---|---|---|---|---|---|---|
| 28 | X | X | X | X | X | X | \ | • | B | X | X | X | X | X | X | 27 |
| 26 | X | X | X | X | X | B | • | ⋀ | • | B | X | X | X | X | X | 25 |
| 24 | X | X | X | X | B | • | / | X | \ | • | B | X | X | X | X | 23 |
| 22 | X | X | X | B | • | / | X | X | X | \ | • | B | X | X | X | 21 |
| 20 | X | X | B | • | / | X | X | X | X | X | \ | • | B | X | X | 19 |
| 18 | X | B | • | / | X | X | X | X | X | X | X | \ | • | B | X | 17 |
| 16 | \ | • | B | X | X | X | X | X | X | X | X | X | B | • | / | 15 |
| 14 | X | \ | • | B | X | X | X | X | X | X | X | B | • | / | X | 13 |
| 12 | X | X | \ | • | B | X | X | X | X | X | B | • | / | X | X | 11 |
| 10 | X | X | X | \ | • | B | X | X | X | B | • | / | X | X | X | 9 |
| 8 | X | X | X | X | \ | • | B | X | B | • | / | X | X | X | X | 7 |
| 6 | X | X | X | X | X | \ | • | B | • | / | X | X | X | X | X | 5 |
| 4 | X | X | X | X | X | X | • | / | X | X | X | X | X | X | X | 3 |
| (WS) 2 | X | X | X | X | X | X | X | X | X | X | X | X | X | X | X | 1 (RS) |

# HOW TO READ CHARTS

Charts are read *exactly* the way you knit. Start at the bottom right hand corner of the chart and read across right to left. Each square on the graph paper represents one completed stitch.

*A Note from Donna*

## MORE ON READING CHARTS

**In circular knitting,** you work in the round, and the right side of the knitting is always facing you. Read all chart rows from right to left.

**In flat knitting,** you work back and forth, turning your work at the end of each row. The first row is worked with the right side of the knitting facing you; the second row is worked with the wrong side facing.

**If only right-side rows are shown on the chart,** you either knit or purl all the way across each wrong-side row. This will be stated in the text.

**If wrong-side rows are shown on the chart:**

- Odd-numbered rows are the right side of the work. Read these rows from right to left.

- Even-numbered rows are the wrong side of the work. Read these rows from left to right.

Even-numbered rows are on the left side of the chart.

Odd-numbered rows are on the right side of the chart.

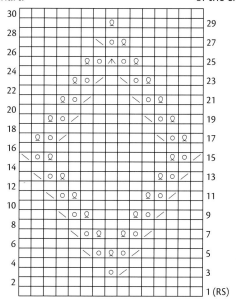

Sometimes both odd-numbered and even-numbered rows are shown.

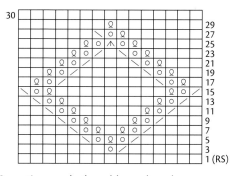

Sometimes only the odd-numbered rows are shown, plus the last even-numbered row.

# Handspun Medallion STOLE

*Designed by Dorothy Reade*

This elegant yet comfortable stole is the last one that
Dorothy Reade designed and knitted, and was unfinished when she died.
Her daughter gave it to Alice Scherp, a good friend of Dorothy's, to finish.
The shawl is special to Alice because it's the only one of Dorothy's shawls that she
has. The shawl is made from handspun yarn designed especially for this project.
Alice graciously allowed me to borrow her treasured stole
and to include the pattern in this book.

**Skill Level:** Intermediate ◼◼◼◻

**Finished Measurements:** 24" wide x 71" long, blocked

## MATERIALS

Handspun 2-ply lace-weight yarn* (100% wool; 275 g; approx 2035 yds)

Size 4 (3.5 mm) circular needle

Tapestry needle

Blocking wires and/or rustproof pins

*The yarn for this stole was handspun by Dorothy. A good substitute would be Jamieson & Smith 2-Ply Lace Yarn.*

**Gauge:** 26 sts and 34 rows = 4" in medallion patt

## INSTRUCTIONS

With A, CO 151 sts.

## Garter Stitch Edge

Knit 12 rows.

## Mesh Pattern

**Next row (RS):** Work 6 sts in garter st, 139 sts in mesh patt (row 1 of chart on page 35), and 6 sts in garter st.

Work patts as established until 6 reps of mesh patt are complete.

## Garter Stitch Frame

**Next row (RS):** Work 6 sts in garter st, 19 sts in mesh patt as established, 101 sts in garter st, 19 sts in mesh patt as established, 6 sts in garter st.

On next row, dec 2 sts in center garter st patt—149 sts.

Work 10 more rows in patts as established.

## Medallion Pattern

**Next row (RS):** Work 6 sts in garter st, 19 sts in mesh patt, 6 sts in garter st, 87 sts of medallion patt (row 1 of chart on page 35), 6 sts in garter st, 19 sts in mesh patt, and 6 sts in garter st.

Work patts as established, working rows 1–4 of medallion patt only once, rep rows 5–18 of medallion patt until 33 reps of the medallion patt have been completed, and then work rows 19–28 once.

## Reverse Pattern for Second End

Rep garter st frame, inc 2 sts in first row of garter sts in center—151 sts. Rep mesh patt and then garter st edge.

BO all sts loosely.

## FINISHING

Weave in ends. Block to dimensions.

## Medallion

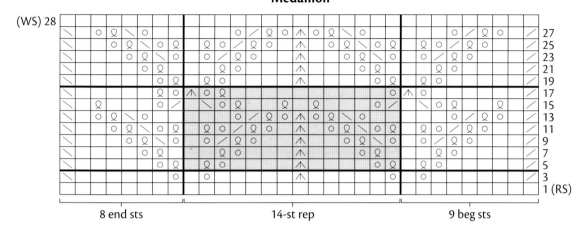

**(WS) 28**

Row numbers on right: 27, 25, 23, 21, 19, 17, 15, 13, 11, 9, 7, 5, 3, 1 (RS)

8 end sts — 14-st rep — 9 beg sts

Work rows 1–4 once.
Rep rows 5–18 a total of 33 times.
Work rows 19–28 once.
Only odd-numbered rows are charted.
Purl all even-numbered rows.

### Mesh

4
2
3
1 (RS)

1 end st — 6-st rep

### Key

| | |
|---|---|
| ☐ K on RS, P on WS | ╲ K2tog tbl or ssk |
| Q K1 tbl | ⋀ sl 1-K2tog-psso |
| ╱ K2tog | ○ YO |

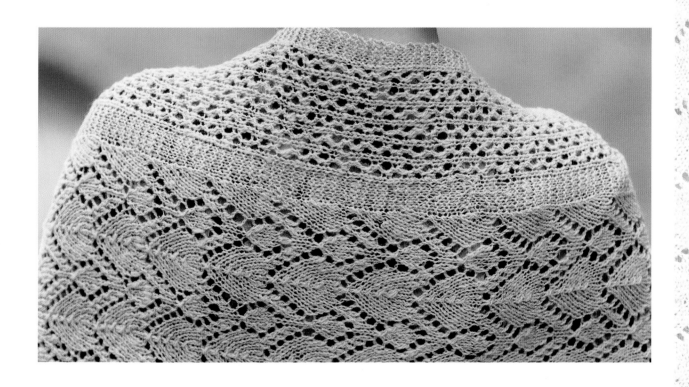

# Eyelet Diamond: SHELL AND STOLE

*Designed by Karin Maag-Tanchak*

A sweet, sleeveless top with side vents!
While any lightweight yarn will work, I selected a silk and merino
yarn for drape and elegance. The rectangular shawl uses chunky-weight
yarn that makes it perfect for a beginning lace knitter.
Big needles and an easy shape will make this project go fast!

## SHELL

**Skill Level:** Intermediate ◖■■▭

**Size:** XS (S, M, L)

**Finished Bust:** 37½ (40, 42¼, 47½)"

**Finished Length:** 21 (22, 23, 24)"

*Note that during blocking, the diamond lace patt will stretch approx ¾" for every 3" knitted. Length may be adjusted during blocking, if desired.*

## MATERIALS

5 (6, 7, 8) skeins of Swirl DK from Lorna's Laces (85% merino, 15% silk; 2 oz; 150 yds) in color 44ns Old Rose

Size 5 (3.75 mm) needles, or size to obtain gauge

Size 4 (3.5 mm) circular needle, 16" long, for neck and armhole edgings

Stitch markers

Stitch holder

Tapestry needle

Blocking wires and/or rustproof pins

**Gauge:** 19 sts and 33 rows = 4" in seed st on larger needles, after blocking

## BACK

With larger needles, CO 89 (95, 101, 113) sts.

Work seed st (see page 110) for 7 rows.

**Next row (WS):** Work seed st for 7 sts, pm, purl to last 7 sts, pm, work seed st to end.

Beg outlined eyelet diamond chart (page 38) between markers, keeping first and last 7 sts in seed st for side slit. Work until piece measures 3", or until two 12-row reps of lace chart have been completed.

Cont patts as established, keeping first and last sts in St st (selvage st), adding 2 more lace reps across row where seed st edging was before.

Work even until piece measures approx 12 (12½, 13, 13)", ending on row 12.

For rem of piece, work rows 11 and 12 of chart only.

**Shape armholes:** Maintaining lace patt, BO 5 (6, 7, 8) sts at beg of next 2 rows, then dec 1 st at both ends of every RS row 6 (6, 6, 8) times—67 (71, 75, 81) sts rem. Cont in patt until armhole measures 8½ (9, 9½, 10½)", ending with row 12.

**Shape shoulders:** Maintaining lace patt, BO 9 (10, 10, 11) sts at beg of next 2 rows, then BO 8 (9, 10, 11) sts at beg of next 2 rows. Put rem 33 (33, 35, 37) sts on st holder.

## FINISHING

Gently block pieces to measurements. Seam sides. Seam shoulders.

Armhole edging: With smaller short circular needle, PU 91 (97, 103, 115) sts. Work in seed st for 6 rnds. BO in patt. Rep on second armhole.

Neck edging: With smaller short circular needle, PU 99 (101, 103, 113) sts around neck edge, working across sts on st holder from back neck edge when you come to them. Work in seed st for 6 rnds. BO in patt.

Gently steam press seams.

### Outlined Eyelet Diamond

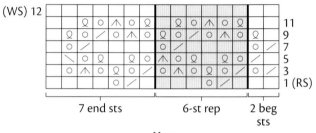

7 end sts    6-st rep    2 beg sts

### Key

| | |
|---|---|
| ☐ | K on RS, P on WS |
| ℧ | K1 tbl |
| ╱ | K2tog |
| ╲ | K2tog tbl or ssk |
| ⋀ | sl 1-K2tog-psso |
| ○ | YO |

Only odd-numbered rows are charted.
Purl all even-numbered rows.

## FRONT

Work as for back, including all shaping, and, AT SAME TIME, when armhole measures 5½ (6, 6½, 7)", beg front neck shaping.

Shape neck: On next RS row, work across 23 (27, 29, 32) sts, attach another ball of yarn, BO center 21 (17, 17, 17) sts, work to end of row.

Working both sides at once, and maintaining patt, dec 1 st at each neck edge, EOR 6 (8, 9, 10) times. Cont in patt until piece measures same as back at beg of shoulder shaping.

Shape shoulders: Work shoulder shaping (at shoulder edge) to correspond with back.

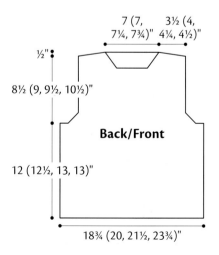

7 (7, 7¼, 7¾)"    3½ (4, 4¼, 4½)"

½"

8½ (9, 9½, 10½)"

**Back/Front**

12 (12½, 13, 13)"

18¾ (20, 21½, 23¾)"

# STOLE

**Skill Level:** Easy ◼◼◻◻

**Finished Measurements:** 24" x 72", after blocking

## MATERIALS

5 skeins of Swirl Chunky from Lorna's Laces (83% merino wool, 17% silk; 100 g; 120 yds) in color 44ns Old Rose **5**

Size 13 (9 mm) needles, or size to obtain gauge

2 stitch markers

Tapestry needle

**Gauge:** 10 sts and 12 rows = 4" in seed st, after blocking

## INSTRUCTIONS

With size 13 needles, CO 55 sts. Work 6 rows seed st (see page 110).

**Next row (WS):** Work seed st for 5 sts, pm, purl next 45 sts, pm, work seed st over last 5 sts.

**Next row (RS):** Keeping first and last 5 sts in seed st, beg regular eyelet diamond chart below over center 45 stitches.

Rep rows 1 through 12 of chart 16 times, or work to desired length. Work rows 1 through 6 of chart once more. Work seed st for 6 rows. BO in patt.

## FINISHING

Weave in ends. Block stole by laying on flat, carpeted surface and misting it with water. Using pins, block to measurements. Allow to dry.

### Regular Eyelet Diamond

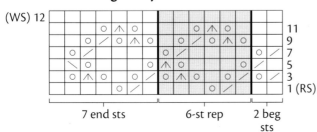

(WS) 12 / 11 / 9 / 7 / 5 / 3 / 1 (RS)

7 end sts    6-st rep    2 beg sts

### Key

| | |
|---|---|
| ☐ | K on RS, P on WS |
| ☒ | K1 tbl |
| ╱ | K2tog |
| ╲ | K2tog tbl or ssk |
| ⋀ | sl 1-K2tog-psso |
| ○ | YO |

Only odd-numbered rows are charted.
Purl all even-numbered rows.

# Diamond Swing TOP
## Designed by Chrissy Gardiner

Flattering to figures of all shapes and sizes,
this versatile design is perfect as a cover-up over a dress
or jeans and also makes a comfy maternity top.

**Skill Level:** Intermediate ◼◼◼▢

**Sizes:** XS (S, M, L, XL)

**Finished Bust:** 32 (36, 40, 44, 48)"

**Finished Length:** 25½ (28, 28½, 32, 33½)"

## MATERIALS

6 (6, 7, 8, 9) skeins of Lion and Lamb from Lorna's Laces (50% wool, 50% silk; 3.5 oz; 205 yds) in color 40ns Sunshine 🔵**4**

Size 8 (5 mm) circular needles, 24" and 16" long, or size to obtain gauge

Extra needle, size 8 (5 mm) or smaller, for three-needle bind off

5 stitch markers (1 a different color)

4 stitch holders or waste yarn

Tapestry needle

2 yards of ribbon (¼" or ⅜" wide) or braided length of yarn

**Gauge:** 18 sts and 24 rows = 4" in St st

## BODY

*This top is completely seamless with sleeves knit from the armholes down for easy fit adjustment.*

With longer circular needle, CO 175 (187, 211, 223, 247) sts. Working back and forth, knit 4 rows.

**Next row (RS):** K3, work first setup row of inset diamonds chart (page 43) to last 3 sts, K3.

**Next row (WS):** K3, work second setup row of chart to last 3 sts, K3.

Keeping first and last 3 sts as K3, work rows 1–16 of chart until body measures 15 (16, 16, 17, 18)". End after working either row 7 or row 15 of chart.

## Bodice

**Dec row (WS):** K5 (6, 5, 7, 7), K2tog, [K1 (3, 3, 4, 4), K2tog] 17 (17, 19, 12, 6) times, [K2 (2, 2, 3, 3), K2tog] 28 (22, 26, 27, 39) times, K5 (6, 5, 7, 7)–129 (147, 165, 183, 201) sts rem.

**Next rnd (RS):** Knit to last 3 sts, pm (the different color) for beg of rnd, place last 3 sts on extra needle and knit them tog with first 3 sts of other end of row as if doing a 3-needle BO, joining body into a rnd–126 (144, 162, 180, 198) sts rem.

**Next rnd:** Purl.

**Eyelet rnd:** *K2tog, YO; rep from * to end of rnd.

Work 3 rnds of garter st as follows: purl, knit, purl.

**Next rnd:** K17 (20, 22, 24, 26), pm for right bust dart, K16 (18, 20, 23, 25), pm for right underarm, K62 (70, 80, 88, 98), pm for left underarm, K16 (18, 20, 23, 25), pm for left bust dart, knit to end of rnd.

Knit 3 more rnds.

**Inc rnd:** *Knit to 1 st before next marker, knit in front and back of next st (inc 1 st), sl marker; rep from * once, **knit to next marker, sl marker, knit in front and back of next st; rep from ** once, knit to end of rnd—130 (148, 166, 184, 202) sts.

Knit 2 (2, 3, 3, 3) more rnds.

Rep the last 3 (3, 4, 4, 4) rnds 3 times—142 (160, 178, 196, 214) sts.

**Next rnd:** Knit to right bust-dart marker, remove marker, knit to 1 st before right underarm marker, K1f&b,sm, knit to left underarm marker, sl marker, K1f&b, knit to left bust-dart marker, remove marker, knit to end of rnd—144 (162, 180, 198, 216) sts.

Work even in St st, if necessary, until bodice measures 3¼ (3¼, 3½, 4½, 5)" from last purl rnd.

## Divide for Front and Back

**Next row (RS):** Remove beg-of-rnd marker, knit to 6 sts before right underarm marker, place next 78 (87, 96, 105, 114) sts on a st holder for underarms and back, leaving underarm markers in place—66 (75, 84, 93, 102) sts rem on needle.

**Next row (WS):** Purl.

Work even in St st until front measures 0 (0, 0, 1, 1)" from underarms.

## Left Front

**Next row (RS):** K29 (33, 38, 42, 47), place next 37 (42, 46, 51, 55) sts on a second st holder for right front.

**Next row (WS):** Purl.

**Dec row (RS):** Knit to last 3 sts, K2tog, K1—28 (32, 37, 41, 46) sts rem.

Work 1 row even.

Rep last 2 rows 4 times—24 (28, 33, 37, 42) sts rem.

Rep dec row once—23 (27, 32, 36, 41) sts rem.

Work 3 rows even.

Rep last 4 rows 2 (1, 4, 3, 4) times—21 (26, 28, 33, 37) sts rem.

Work even until armhole measures 6½ (8, 8, 9½, 9½)". End after working a WS row. Place rem sts on st holder for left shoulder.

## Right Front

**Next row (RS):** With RS facing you and leaving first 8 (9, 8, 9, 8) sts on holder for center of neck, place rem 29 (33, 38, 42, 47) right-front sts on needle, join yarn at neck edge and knit across.

**Next row (WS):** Purl.

**Dec row (RS):** K1, ssk, knit to end of row—28 (32, 37, 41, 46) sts rem.

Work 1 row even.

Rep last 2 rows 4 times—24 (28, 33, 37, 42) sts rem.

Rep dec row once—23 (27, 32, 36, 41) sts rem.

Work 3 rows even.

Rep last 4 rows 2 (1, 4, 3, 4) times—21 (26, 28, 33, 37) sts rem.

Work even until armhole measures 6½ (8, 8, 9½, 9½)". End after working a WS row. Place rem sts on st holder for right shoulder.

## Upper Back

Place first and last 6 sts from back-body holder onto smaller holders for underarms. Place rem 66 (75, 84, 93, 102) sts on needle, join yarn at right edge of back and knit across. Work even until back measures same as front, ending with a WS row.

## Join Shoulders

With RS tog, join shoulders using 3-needle BO starting at outer edge and working in toward neck. Leave rem 24 (23, 28, 27, 28) sts from back on st holder for back neck.

## SLEEVES

Place 3 leftmost underarm sts from underarm holder onto shorter circular needle. Join yarn and, starting at underarm with same needle, PU 55 (67, 67, 79, 79) sts evenly around armhole, then knit rem 3 sts from holder onto needle—61 (73, 73, 85, 85) sleeve sts. Pm to indicate beg of rnd.

Work rows 1–16 of inset diamonds chart across all sleeve sts in the rnd until sleeve measures 15 (14, 14, 13, 13)" from armhole. End with patt row 7 or row 15 of chart.

**Next rnd:** Knit.

**Next rnd:** Purl.

Rep last 2 rnds 2 times.

BO all sts. Fasten off.

Rep for second sleeve.

## FINISHING

**Neckband:** Place back neck sts on longer needle and knit across them. PU 3 sts for every 4 rows down left-front edge of neckline. Knit across 8 (9, 8, 9, 8) front neck sts. PU sts along right-front edge of neckline as for left front. Pm to indicate beg of rnd. Work 5 rnds in garter st. BO all sts. Weave in ends. Block to dimensions. Thread a ribbon or braided length of yarn through eyelets at bottom edge of bodice and tie in front.

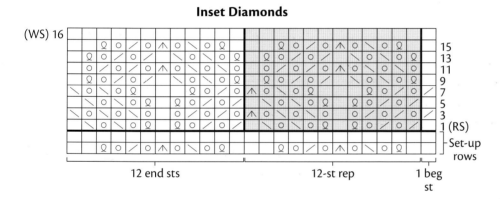

**Inset Diamonds**

(WS) 16

15
13
11
9
7
5
3
1 (RS)

Set-up rows

12 end sts          12-st rep          1 beg st

**Key**

K on RS, P on WS
Ꝗ K1 tbl
∕ K2tog
∖ K2tog tbl or ssk
⋀ sl 1-K2tog-psso
○ YO

Only odd-numbered rows are charted. When working back and forth on body, purl all even-numbered rows. When working in the rnd on sleeve, knit all even-numbered rows.

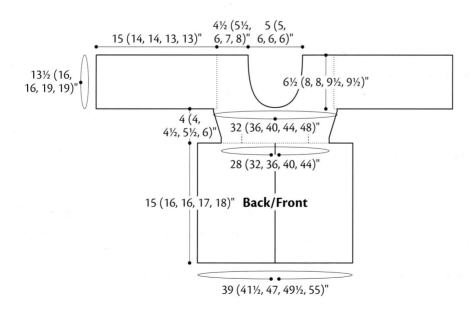

15 (14, 14, 13, 13)"     4½ (5½, 6, 7, 8)"     5 (5, 6, 6, 6)"

13½ (16, 16, 19, 19)"

6½ (8, 8, 9½, 9½)"

4 (4, 4½, 5½, 6)"

32 (36, 40, 44, 48)"

28 (32, 36, 40, 44)"

15 (16, 16, 17, 18)"  **Back/Front**

39 (41½, 47, 49½, 55)"

Bottom of body is knit back and forth.

# Beaded HAND WARMERS and SOCKS
### *Designed by Jackie Erickson-Schweitzer*

So delicate and exquisite, the beauty of lace combined with tiny beads! The graceful lines of Dorothy Reade's offset-chevrons pattern are embellished with sparkling beads in these eye-catching matchups for hands and feet. Make either the Hand Warmers or the Socks, or whip up a cozy set for yourself. They make great gifts that are sure to be well received, too.

**Skill Level:** Experienced ■■■■

**Size:** Women's Medium

**Finished Hand Warmer Measurements**
Circumference around scalloped cuff edge: 8"
Circumference around ribbed wrist
(not stretched): 5½"

**Finished Sock Measurements**
Circumference around scalloped cuff edge: 8"
Leg length from top of heel to edge of cuff: 5½"
Foot circumference: 7½"
Foot length: 9½"

## MATERIALS
### Hand Warmers

1 skein of Shepherd Sock from Lorna's Laces (80% Superwash wool, 20% nylon; 2 oz; 215 yds) in color 34 Tahoe **1**

554 size 8/0 Miyuki glass seed beads in color 18 Silver-lined Light Blue

### Socks

2 skeins of Shepherd Sock from Lorna's Laces in color 34 Tahoe **1**

554 size 8/0 Miyuki glass seed beads in color 18 Silver-lined Light Blue

### For Both Hand Warmers and Socks

Size 1 (2.25 mm) needles, or size to obtain gauge, your choice of double pointed or circular

Dental-floss threader, split-eye beading needle, or similar for stringing beads onto yarn

2 stitch markers

Tapestry needle

Stitch holder

### Gauge

30½ sts and 48 rnds = 4" over beaded offset-chevrons patt

32 sts and 48 rnds = 4" over St st

## PATTERN STITCH
### Twisted Ribbing

(Multiple of 2 sts)

**All rnds:** K1tbl, P1.

## SPECIAL TECHNIQUE
### Slide Bead

Slide a bead along yarn so that it's next to needle at last st worked. Work next st as instructed, taking care that bead rem in place on running thread between sts at front of fabric and is not pulled through loop while making the new st.

## BEADED CUFF INSTRUCTIONS

*This is a common set of instructions used in making the hand warmers or the start of the socks.*

With yarn, thread small tapestry needle that can accommodate the yarn and still pass through holes in beads. String 277 beads onto yarn for one cuff. As you knit, slide beads down along yarn until needed. Since there are many beads to begin with, be careful to push along beads in sections of only a few inches at a time.

CO 61 sts loosely.

**Foundation row:** Sl 1 pw wyib, knit to last st, P1.

Distribute sts to beg knitting circularly. Being careful not to twist sts, join into rnd, pm to mark center back of sock leg or center palm of hand warmer.

**Beaded edging rnd 1 (61 beads to be used):** *Slide bead, P1; rep from * to end of rnd.

**Foundation rnd:** Knit.

**Rnds 1–32:** Work rnds 1–8 of beaded offset chevrons chart on facing page 4 times for a total of 32 rnds. You'll be working the 20-st multiple 3 times in each rnd.

Work rnds 33–41 of beaded offset chevrons transition into twisting ribbing chart on facing page.

Work twisted ribbing for 2".

## BEADED HAND WARMERS

Follow the beaded cuff instructions at left.

BO loosely in twisted ribbing patt.

**Finishing:** Weave in ends. Wash and lightly block by stretching the lace areas with your fingers.

## BEADED SOCKS

Follow the beaded cuff instructions at left.

### Divide for Heel

Work 15 sts in twisted ribbing. These 15 sts and previous 14 sts will be worked for heel. Put these 29 sts on one needle for heel flap. Put rem 31 sts on a st holder for instep.

### Heel Flap

Working back and forth in rows on heel sts only, turn.

**Row 1 (WS):** Sl 1 pw wyif, purl across.

**Row 2 (RS):** (Sl 1 pw wyib, K1) 14 times, K1.

Rep these 2 rows until heel flap measures 2½", or until heel reaches the depth desired, ending with a RS row.

### Heel Turn

**Row 1 (WS):** Sl 1 pw wyif, P15, P2tog, P1, turn work.

**Row 2 (RS):** Sl 1 pw wyib, K4, ssk, K1, turn.

**Row 3 (WS):** Sl 1 pw wyif, P5, P2tog, P1, turn.

**Row 4 (RS):** Sl 1 pw wyib, K6, ssk, K1, turn.

Cont as established, working 1 more st between sl 1 and dec in each row, until you've completed a RS row in which all sts have been worked. Do not turn after final row—17 sts.

## Gusset and Foot

Working in the rnd, PU 1 st into each slipped st along side of heel flap. Count how many sts you picked up. Pm to mark beg of instep and end of rnd. Place held instep sts on needle and work across in established twisted-ribbing patt. Pm to mark end of instep. PU same number of sts along other edge of heel flap as first. Knit to end of rnd.

**Rnd 1:** Work across instep in established patt to second marker, sm, K2tog, knit to 2 sts from end-of-rnd marker, ssk—2 sts dec.

**Rnd 2:** Work in established patt.

Rep gusset rnds 1 and 2 until 60 sts rem. Cont without dec in established patt until foot of sock as measured from back of heel is 8" or 1½" shorter than desired foot length.

## Toe

**Rnd 1:** K1, ssk, knit to 3 sts from second marker, K2tog, K1, sm, knit to end-of-rnd marker.

**Rnd 2:** Knit.

**Rnd 3:** K1, ssk, knit to 3 sts from second marker, K2tog, K1, sm, K1, ssk, knit to 3 sts from end-of-rnd marker, K2tog, K1.

Rep rnds 2 and 3 until 30 sts rem and rnd 2 completed.

Rep rnd 3 until 18 sts rem.

## Finishing

Join toe sts with Kitchener st (see page 110). Weave in ends. Wash and lightly block by stretching the lace areas with your fingers.

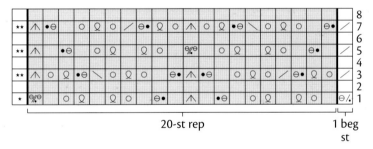

**Beaded Offset Chevrons**

20-st rep · 1 beg st

**Beaded Offset Chevrons Transition into Twisted Ribbing**

20-st rep · 1 beg st

### Key

| | | |
|---|---|---|
| ☐ K | ⋏ sl 1-K2tog-psso | ★ Substitute ⟋⊖ for last ⊘⋰⊖ of the round. |
| • P | ⊖• P1, slide bead | ★★ Substitute ⟍ for last ⋏ of the round. |
| ○ YO | •⊖ Slide bead, P1 | ★★★ Substitute ⟋⋰ for last • of the round (i.e., remove |
| ℚ K1 tbl | ⟋⊖ Slide bead, P2tog | end-of-round marker, purl last stitch of round with |
| ⟍ K2tog tbl or ssk | ⊖⟋ P2tog, slide bead | next stitch, replace marker at current position). |
| ⟋ K2tog | ⊘⋰⊖ Slide bead, P3tog, slide bead | |
| ⟋⋰ P2tog | | |

# Time for Tea: TEA COZY and TABLE RUNNER
## *Designed by Ava Coleman*

Afternoon tea is fun, especially when it's shared
with special people. This tea cozy and table runner were inspired
by a family gathering with four generations of knitters.

**Skill Level:** Easy ●■□□

**Finished Measurements**
Cozy (measured flat at longest and widest
points): 9" x 10"
Table Runner: 12" x 48"

## MATERIALS

5 skeins of Adagio Fingering Yarn from Yarn Place
(100% wool; 50 g; 218 yds) in color 689208 **2**

Size 6 (4 mm) needles, or size to obtain gauge

Tapestry needle

**Gauge:** 20 sts and 24 rows = 4" in lace patt

## TEA COZY

*The tea cozy is made of 2 identical pieces that
are joined, leaving an opening for the spout and
handle.*

CO 51 sts.

**Setup row:** Knit.

**Row 1 (RS):** Sl 1, K3, work row 1 of solid and open
waves chart (page 50), K3, K1tbl.

**Row 2 (WS):** Sl 1, K3, purl to last 4 sts, K3, K1tbl.

Keeping first and last 4 sts as established, work
rows 1–24 of chart twice, then work rows 1–4 one
more time for a total of 52 rows of chart.

Work rows 53–64 of open waves dec chart
(page 50).

**Rows 65–67:** Knit.

BO all sts.

Rep for second piece.

## Finishing

Weave in ends. Wash and block pieces, then sew
tog at sides, leaving openings for handle and spout.

## TABLE RUNNER

CO 61 sts.

Work in garter st for 12".

Beg working solid and open waves chart (page 50)
as follows:

*Row 1 (RS): Sl 1, K1, work chart row 1, K1, K1tbl.

Row 2 (WS): Sl 1, K1, purl to last 2 sts, K1, K1tbl.

Keeping first and last 2 sts as established, work all
rows of chart 9 times.

Knit 3 rows. BO all sts.*

Pick up 61 sts along cast on edge. Work from * to
* to correspond with other side.

## Finishing

Weave in ends. Block to dimensions.

## Solid and Open Waves

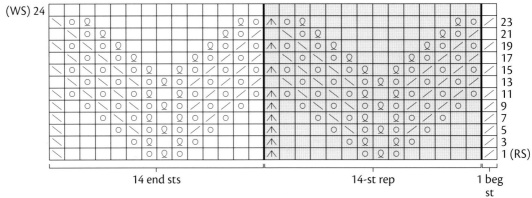

14 end sts    14-st rep    1 beg st

Only odd-numbered rows are charted.
Purl all even-numbered rows.

## Open Waves Decrease

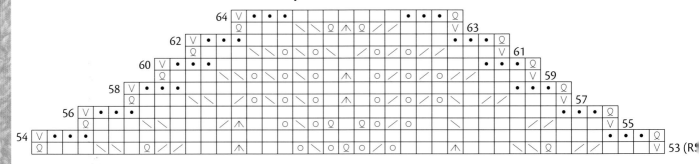

## Key

| | |
|---|---|
| ☐ | K on RS, P on WS |
| • | P on RS, K on WS |
| Ϙ | K1 tbl |
| ╱ | K2tog |
| ╲ | K2tog tbl or ssk |
| V | sl 1 |
| ⋀ | sl 1-K2tog-psso |
| ○ | YO |

# Mendocino SOCKS
*Designed by Kristi Schueler*

These feminine lace socks are knit at a fine gauge
with a unique mirrored gusset placement.

**Skill Level:** Experienced ■■■◼

**Sizes:** Child's 12–13 (Women's 3–4, Women's 5–6,
Women's 7–8, Women's 9–10)

**Finished Sock Circumference:** 6½ (7, 7¼, 7¾, 8)"*

**Finished Foot Length:** 7½ (7¾, 8¼, 8¾, 9½)"

*These socks use an unconventional gusset and
heel formation that requires more negative ease
than standard socks. While the construction makes
the socks look large, once the heel is completed
the fit should be fine if you matched gauge and
incorporated the appropriate ease.*

## MATERIALS

MC  1 skein of Pro Natura Sock Yarn from Zitron
Trekking (75% wool, 25% unprocessed
bamboo; 3.5 oz/100 g; 459 yds/420 m) in
color 1511 Light Blue (1)

CC  1 skein of Pro Natura Sock Yarn from Zitron
Trekking in color 1535 Ivory (1)

2 circular needles*, size 0 (2.0 mm), 16" long, or
size to obtain gauge

1 locking stitch marker or safety pin

4 stitch markers

Tapestry needle

*The pattern is written specifically for knitting on
two circular needles. If you wish to knit with double-
pointed needles, simply substitute needles 1 and 2
for needle 1 and needles 3 and 4 for needle 2.*

**Gauge:** 40 sts and 52 rnds = 4" over St st

## TOE

CO 6 sts using Turkish CO, with 3 sts on each
circular needle as follows:

Align ends of two separate circular needles and
place in left hand. Take end of yarn and create
slipknot over bottom needle. CO by wrapping
working yarn to the **back** and **up** and **over**; then
**down** the front and **under both** needles. Rep
looping process over both needles 2 more times
for total of 3 sts on each needle. Pull tip of bottom
needle to the right so that loops rest on cable of
bottom needle. Place other end of top needle
into right hand and knit the loops. Pull top needle
to left so sts just knit rest on the cable. Turn work
clockwise. Push loops on cable of bottom needle up
onto needle tip. The slipknot will be first st. Let that
fall off tip of needle. Knit loops on this needle as
you did before. The first and last sts should be knit
through back loop to prevent those sts from being
twisted. Move sts just knit onto cable of its needle
and turn work clockwise once again. Knit across sts
on top of first needle you knit once again.

Needle 1 holds sole sts and needle 2 holds instep
sts. Use locking st marker or safety pin to mark
needle 1.

**Rnd 1:** *LRinc, K1; rep from * 5 times—12 sts.

**Rnd 2:** On needle 1, (K2, pm) twice, K2. On needle
2, (K2, pm) twice, K2.

**Rnd 3:** *LRinc, knit to marker, sm, LRinc, knit to marker, sm, LRinc, knit to end of needle; rep from * once for needle 2—18 sts.

**Rnd 4:** Knit.

Rep rnds 3 and 4 until total stitch count equals 60 (66, 72, 72, 78).

Rep rnd 3, inc in only 4 (2, 0, 4, 2) sections as established, distributing as evenly as possible for 64 (68, 72, 76, 80) total sts. Remove markers.

**Rnd 5 of right sock:** Knit sts on needle 1. On needle 2, K1, work pebble lace panel (page 57) over next 9 sts, knit to end of rnd.

**Rnd 5 of left sock:** Knit sts on needle 1. On needle 2, knit to last 10 sts, work pebble lace panel over next 9 sts, K1.

Rep appropriate rnd 5 until toe measures 2½ (2½, 2¾, 3, 3½)".

## GUSSET

### Right Sock

**Rnd 1:** On needle 1 (sole), K31 (33, 35, 37, 39), pm, K1f&b. On needle 2 (instep), K1, pm, cont pebble lace panel as established, knit to end of rnd—65 (69, 73, 77, 81) sts.

**Rnd 2:** Knit.

**Rnd 3:** Knit to marker, sm, K1, LLinc, K1, LRinc, K1, sm, work pebble lace panel over next 9 sts, knit to end of rnd—67 (71, 75, 79, 83) sts.

**Rnds 4 and 5:** Knit.

**Rnd 6:** Knit to marker, sm, K1, LLinc, knit to 1 st before second marker, LRinc, K1, sm, work pebble lace panel over next 9 sts, knit to end of rnd—69 (73, 77, 81, 85) sts.

### Left Sock

**Rnd 1:** On needle 1 (sole), K1, pm, K31 (33, 35, 37, 39). On needle 2 (instep), K22 (24, 26, 28, 30), work pebble lace panel as established, pm, K1f&b—65 (69, 73, 77, 81) sts.

**Rnd 2:** Knit.

**Rnd 3:** Knit to 1 st before marker, LRinc, K1, sm, work pebble lace panel over next 9 sts, sm, K1, LLinc, knit to end of rnd—67 (71, 75, 79, 83) sts.

**Rnds 4 and 5:** Knit.

**Rnd 6:** Knit to 1 st before marker, LRinc, K1, sm, work pebble lace panel over next 9 sts, sm, K1, LLinc, knit to end of rnd—69 (73, 77, 81, 85) sts.

### For Both Socks

Rep appropriate rnds 4–6 above until total sts equal 95 (101, 107, 113, 119) at end of rnd 6.

**Right sock heel setup rnd:** Knit across needle 1, moving marker 10 sts to the left. Cont knitting onto needle 1 from needle 2 to 15 (16, 17, 18, 19) sts past pebble lace panel, moving second marker to end of panel. Knit next 33 (35, 37, 39, 41) sts onto needle 2. Sl rem sts to needle 1. The working yarn should now be at end of needle 2, which now holds heel/sole sts.

**Needle 1:** 15 (16, 17, 18, 19) sts, marker, 23 (25, 27, 29, 31) sts, 9 pebble lace panel sts, marker, 15 (16, 17, 18, 19) sts.

**Needle 2:** 33 (35, 37, 39, 41).

**Left sock heel setup rnd:** Pm as indicated, removing old ones as you reach them. K6 (7, 8, 9, 10), pm, K15 (16, 17, 18, 19) onto needle 1. Knit next 33 (35, 37, 39, 41) sts onto needle 2. Sl rem sts on needle 2 to needle 1, pm to right of pebble lace panel. The working yarn should now be at end of needle 2, which now holds heel/sole sts.

**Needle 1:** 15 (16, 17, 18, 19) sts, marker, 9 pebble lace panel sts, 23 (25, 27, 29, 31) sts, marker, 15 (16, 17, 18, 19) sts.

Needle 2: 33 (35, 37, 39, 41).

Note that needle 1 holds the instep/front of leg sts and needle 2 holds the heel/sole/back of leg sts. It will cont as such for the remainder of the patt.

## HEEL

Knit across needle 1, working 5 (5, 6, 6, 6) evenly distributed LRincs in section before first marker. Knit center section, cont pebble lace panel as established, knit rem section of instep sts, working 5 (5, 6, 6, 6) evenly distributed LLincs—105 (111, 119, 125, 131) sts total.

Needle 1: 20 (21, 23, 24, 25) sts, marker, 32 (34, 36, 38, 40) sts, marker, 20 (21, 23, 24, 25) sts.

Needle 2: 33 (35, 37, 39, 41).

Knit heel back and forth on needle 2 only as follows.

Row 1 (RS): Knit to last 2 sts, w&t.

Row 2 (WS): Purl to last 2 sts, w&t.

Row 3: Knit to 1 st before previously wrapped st, w&t.

Row 4: Purl to 1 st before previously wrapped st, w&t.

Rep rows 3 and 4 until 9 (9, 10, 11, 12) sts are wrapped on each side, ending after row 4.

Row 5 (RS): Knit to first wrapped st, *cw; rep from * until 1 wrapped st rem, cw/ssk, turn.

Row 6 (WS): Sl 1, purl to first wrapped st, *cw; rep from * until 1 wrapped st rem, cw/P2tog. Needle 2: 31 (33, 35, 37, 39) sts.

## BACK OF HEEL

With RS of needle 2 facing you, sl first and last 20 (21, 23, 24, 25) sts from beg and end of needle 1 to needle 2, pm to identify original needle 2 sts.

Needle 1: 32 (34, 36, 38, 40) sts.

Needle 2: 20 (21, 23, 24, 25) sts, pm, 31 (33, 35, 37, 39) sts, pm, 20 (21, 23, 24, 25) sts—103 (109, 117, 123, 129) total sts.

To access working yarn, sl all sts to right of working yarn onto other end of needle 2 as though just worked. Both tips of needle 2 are now at right-most gap, with the working yarn coming from first st on left needle tip.

Cont to work flat on needle 2 only.

Row 7 (RS): Sl 1, knit to 1 st before marker, remove marker and ssk across gap, turn.

Row 8 (WS): Sl 1, purl to 1 st before marker, remove marker and P2tog across gap, turn.

Row 9: Sl 1, knit to 1 st before gap, ssk across gap, turn.

Rows 10: Sl 1, purl to 1 st before gap, P2tog across gap, turn.

Rep rows 9 and 10 until 2 sts rem to the outside of each gap.

Next row (RS): Sl 1, knit to 1 st before gap, ssk, k1.

Next row: Resume knitting in the rnd by knitting across needle 1, cont pebble lace panel as established. On needle 2, K1, K2tog, knit to end of rnd—65 (69, 73, 77, 81) sts.

Needle 1: 32 (34, 36, 38, 40) sts.

Needle 2: 33 (35, 37, 39, 41) sts.

## LEG (FOR BOTH SOCKS)

Cont knitting leg of sock straight with pebble lace panel as established. Stop and move to cuff after completion of rnd 8 of the 9th pebble on the sock.

## CUFF SETUP

On next rnd, work inc as given below for your size and sock.

Right sock Child's 12-13: K12, LLinc, K11, LLinc, K14 working pebble lace panel as established, LLinc, (K14, LLinc) twice—70 sts.

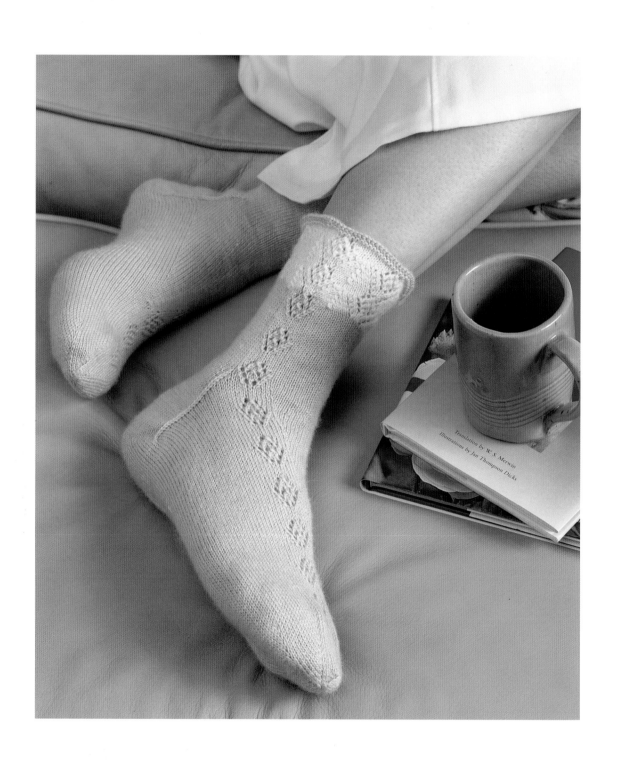

**Left sock Child's 12–13:** Work pebble lace panel as established, LLinc, (K14, LLinc) 4 times—70 sts.

**Right and left socks Women's 3–4:** Knit to end of rnd, work pebble lace panel as established, LLinc—70 sts.

**Right sock Women's 5–6:** (K7, LLinc) twice, (K6, LLinc) twice, K11 working pebble lace panel as established, LLinc, (K6, LLinc) 6 times—84 sts.

**Left sock Women's 5–6:** Work pebble lace panel as established, LLinc, (K7, LLinc) 3 times, (K6, LLinc) 6 times, K7, LLinc—84 sts.

**Right sock Women's 7–8:** K12, LLinc, K13, LLinc, K13 working pebble lace panel as established, LLinc, K9, LLinc, (K10, LLinc) 3 times—84 sts.

**Left sock Women's 7–8:** K11 working pebble lace panel as established, LLinc, (K11, LLinc) 6 more times—84 sts.

**Right and left socks Women's 9–10:** (K27 working pebble lace panel as established, LLinc) 3 times—84 sts.

With CC, knit 1 rnd, moving start of rnd to align pebble lace panels with cuff pattern as given for your size and sock. If markers were used to identify the lace panel, remove them on this rnd.

**Right sock Child's 12–13 and Women's 3–4:** Move start of rnd 3 sts to the left by knitting first 3 sts on needle 1 onto end of needle 2 at end of rnd.

**Right sock Women's 5–6:** Move start of rnd 4 sts to the right by knitting to last 4 sts of rnd, sl 4 sts at end of needle 2 to beg of needle 1.

**Right sock Women's 7–8 and Women's 9–10:** Move start of rnd 5 sts to the right by knitting to last 5 sts of rnd, sl 5 sts at end of needle 2 to beg of needle 1.

**Left sock all sizes:** Move start of rnd 6 sts to the left by knitting first 6 sts on needle 1 onto end of needle 2 at end of rnd.

## CUFF

Beg pebble and shell chart. There will be 5 (5, 6, 6, 6) reps in a rnd. Move sts between needles as required to avoid dec or YOs across needles. Knit 14 rows of chart twice.

Change to MC. Knit 1 rnd. Purl 1 rnd. Knit 1 rnd. BO all sts very loosely.

## FINISHING

Weave in ends. Wash and block.

**Pebble Lace Panel**

Only odd-numbered rnds are charted.
Knit all even-numbered rnds.

**Pebble and Shell**

**Key**

| | |
|---|---|
| ☐ | K |
| Q | K1 tbl |
| / | K2tog |
| \ | K2tog tbl or ssk |
| ⋀ | sl 1-K2tog-psso |
| ○ | YO |
| ▓ | No st |

Note that pebble and shell pattern travels.

Yellow shaded sts should not be knit on last rep of rnd and instead should be slipped to the beg of the rnd.

# Bronte Victorian Jacket
*Designed by Marnie MacLean*

This is an updated take on a Victorian-style jacket, meant to be both flattering and comfortable. Darts and short rows allow for customization, and the near-seamless construction means almost no finishing.

**Skill Level:** Experienced ■■■■

**Size:** XXS (XS, S, M, L, XL)

**Finished Bust:** 31 (32½, 38, 39½, 45¼, 49¼)"

**Finished Length:** 26 (26½, 27, 27¾, 28¼, 28¾)"

## MATERIALS

6 (6, 7, 7, 8, 8) skeins of Lion and Lamb from Lorna's Laces (50% wool, 50% silk; 3.5 oz; 205 yards) in color 49ns Periwinkle

Size 7 (4.5 mm) circular needle, 36" or 44" long, or size to obtain gauge

Size 7 (4.5 mm) set of 5 double-pointed needles

6 stitch markers (2 should be a different color)

Stitch holders

Tapestry needle

7 or more buttons, ⅜" diameter

Sewing needle and matching thread

**Gauge:** 20 sts and 26 rows = 4" over St st

## BODY

*The front and back are knit in one piece to the underarms, then split for the armholes and joined at the shoulders with a 3-needle BO.*

*Read all of the body instructions before beginning, because several shaping operations are completed AT THE SAME TIME.*

Using a provisional cast on, CO 137 (149, 173, 185, 209, 233) sts. Place side seam markers 30 (33, 39, 42, 48, 54) sts from each end of CO row, with 77 (83, 95, 101, 113, 125) sts between markers for the back. With different color or size st markers, mark front darts by placing st markers 19 (21, 23, 25, 28, 31) sts from side seams. Mark the back darts by placing st markers 25 (28, 32, 35, 38, 42) sts from side seams.

### Lower Body

Front and back darts are identical but the rows they beg on vary.

- Dart decs are worked as follows: Work to 2 sts before dart st marker, K2tog (or ssp on purl side), sm, ssk (or P2tog on purl side).

- Dart incs are worked as follows: Work to st marker, lift st from below last st worked, knit (or purl on purl side) lifted st, sm, pick up st below next st to be worked, knit (or purl on purl side) lifted st. Rep for each subsequent dart.

Work 4 (4, 4, 6, 8, 9) rows even, then work back darts as follows: Dec on first row and every 7th row for a total of 5 sets of decs—57 (63, 75, 81, 93, 105) sts in back section.

AT THE SAME TIME, on the 10th row of the back dart shaping, work the front darts as follows: Dec on first row and every 5th row for a total of 5 sets of decs. The rem of the dart is identical to the back dart.

When back and front darts are complete, you will have worked 39 (39, 39, 41, 43, 44) rows. Work 7 rows even—46 (46, 46, 48, 50, 51) rows completed.

Beg working top darts (front and back) as follows: Inc on next and every 8th row for a total of 5 sets of incs. You now have the same number of sts in the back section as you did in your original CO. Darts end on row 87 (87, 87, 89, 91, 92). Remove front and back dart markers.

## Shape Neck

AT THE SAME TIME, beg shaping neck as follows: Work 1 st in patt, ssk (on knit side) or P2tog (on purl side), work to last 3 sts, K2tog (on knit side) or ssp (on purl side), work last st in patt. Dec once at neckline, starting on row 59 (59, 59, 59, 59, 59), then every 11 (11, 12, 12, 11, 11) rows 4 (1, 7, 4, 3, 1) times. Then every 12 (12, 0, 13, 12, 12) rows 3 (6, 0, 3, 5, 7) times. Work neckline even until end of garment.

## Bust Darts

IMMEDIATELY AFTER body darts are finished, and AT THE SAME TIME as neckline shaping, beg working short-row bust darts as follows:

> **Dart Note:** Bust dart assumes a B cup. Add additional rows for larger bust, or omit if you do not require the extra shaping. Bust darts are worked only on the front sections of the garment and each front is worked independently. Work the bust dart for the front section at the beg of your current row, complete it, knit across to the other end of the row, turn your work, and start the other dart. Bust darts are not counted in total row count.

Work to 5 (6, 6, 7, 8, 9) sts before side seam, w&t. Work back to end of row.

Work to 9 (11, 12, 14, 15, 17) sts before side seam, w&t. Work back to end of row.

Work to 14 (16, 18, 21, 23, 26) sts before side seam, w&t. Work back to end of row.

Work to end of row and work bust dart on other front section.

Cont working all sections at once. Pick up and knit all wraps as you go.

Work 15 (20, 15, 13, 13, 17) rows even.

Work each section separately. Remember to work decs at neck edge while working rem rows.

## Divide for Fronts and Back

AT THE SAME TIME, on row 102 (102, 101, 101, 99, 99), beg working armholes as follows: Work to 2 (3, 3, 4, 4, 4) sts before side seam, BO 4 (6, 6, 8, 8, 8) sts. Rep at next side seam. Working back and fronts separately, cont armhole decs as follows (indicated on back but fronts are worked the same):

**Dec row (RS):** Sl 1, ssk, work to last 3 sts, K2tog, K1.

**Dec row (WS):** Sl 1, P2tog, work to last 3 sts, ssp, P1.

Work armhole decs every row 1 (1, 2, 2, 3, 4) time, then EOR 3 (2, 7, 6, 8, 10) times. Cont to work fronts, shaping neck and armholes AT THE SAME TIME as indicated above.

## Upper Back

Work even to row 140 (142, 143, 146, 149, 151).

On row 141 (143, 144, 147, 150, 152), BO center 29 (28, 34, 33, 38, 41) sts.

Back is now worked in two separate pieces. On neck edge, dec 1 st every row for 4 rows.

AFTER back neck on row 145 (147, 148, 151, 154, 156), there should be 16 (19, 19, 22, 24, 27) sts rem for each shoulder. Shape shoulders, beg next row at neckline edge, as follows:

Work to 4 (4, 3, 4, 4, 4) sts before armhole edge, w&t. Work back to neck.

Work to 8 (8, 6, 8, 8, 8) sts before armhole edge, w&t. Work back to neck.

Work to 12 (12, 9, 12, 12, 12) sts before armhole edge, w&t. Work back to neck.

Work to 0 (0, 20, 20, 24, 24) sts before armhole edge, w&t. Work back to neck.

Work to 0 (0, 0, 0, 20, 20) sts before armhole edge, w&t. Work back to neck.

## Upper Fronts

Cont working armhole even and shaping neckline in established patt. When armholes measure the same as back to shoulder, shape shoulders as for back.

Join shoulders with 3-needle BO, picking up any rem wraps.

## SLEEVES

Using circular needles or dpns, PU 52 (60, 64, 72, 76, 82) sts around one armhole, starting at point where side seam would be for front and back. Make sure to mark center top point (where shoulder seam is) and have the same number of sts on either side of armhole. Knit 1 rnd even.

K35 (40, 43, 48, 50, 55) sts (approx two thirds the total number of sts), w&t.

P18 (20, 22, 24, 26, 28) sts (approx one third the total number of sts), w&t.

Knit to 1 st past last w&t on this side, picking up and working wraps as you get to them, w&t.

Purl to 1 st past last w&t on this side, picking up and working wraps as you get to them, w&t.

Rep last 2 rows until you have worked all but last 4 (6, 6, 8, 8, 8) sts, which is 2 (3, 3, 4, 4, 5) sts on either side of marker (same as the total number of underarm BO sts from body).

Work 1 complete rnd even.

Dec rnd: Ssk, work to 2 sts before end of rnd, K2tog.

Work dec rnd 7 (5, 7, 11, 13, 16) more times over next 109 (112, 115, 118, 117, 115) rows—36 (48, 48, 48, 48, 48).

Cuff: Work sleeve lace chart on facing page for one and a half vertical reps (30 rnds).

Work picot BO.

## HEM

Leave long tails for seaming the corners.

Remove provisional CO—137 (149, 173, 185, 209, 233) sts. Starting on WS, purl 1 row. Work rows 1–30 of hem lace chart once.

Work picot BO as follows: BO 2 sts, *move st from right needle to left needle. CO 1 st by placing needle into last st worked, pulling up loop as if to knit and placing it on left needle, BO 3 sts beg with st you just made, rep from * to end of row.

## FINISHING

Button band and collar: Lay out the garment so that RS is facing you. PU 1 st in lower-right corner of garment. This should be the same spot as edge of hem. Cont picking up sts all the way around garment, approx 2 sts for every 3 rows and 1 st for every st across back neck. You need a final number of sts that is a multiple of 12 sts + 5 sts, ending with your last st in the opposite corner. Using this general formula, PU a total of 233 (233, 245, 257, 269, 269) sts. Turn so that WS is facing and purl 1 row. Work 30 rows of hem lace chart on facing page. Work picot BO above. Wash and block. It's easier to block the hem and button band before you seam it. Seam corners of hem to corners of button band. Weave in ends.

Closures: Try on the garment and determine how many closures you'd like and where you'd like them to go. The sample garment has seven buttons, placed at every other lace peak from neck to hem. You may opt to add more or fewer buttons.

**Hem Lace**

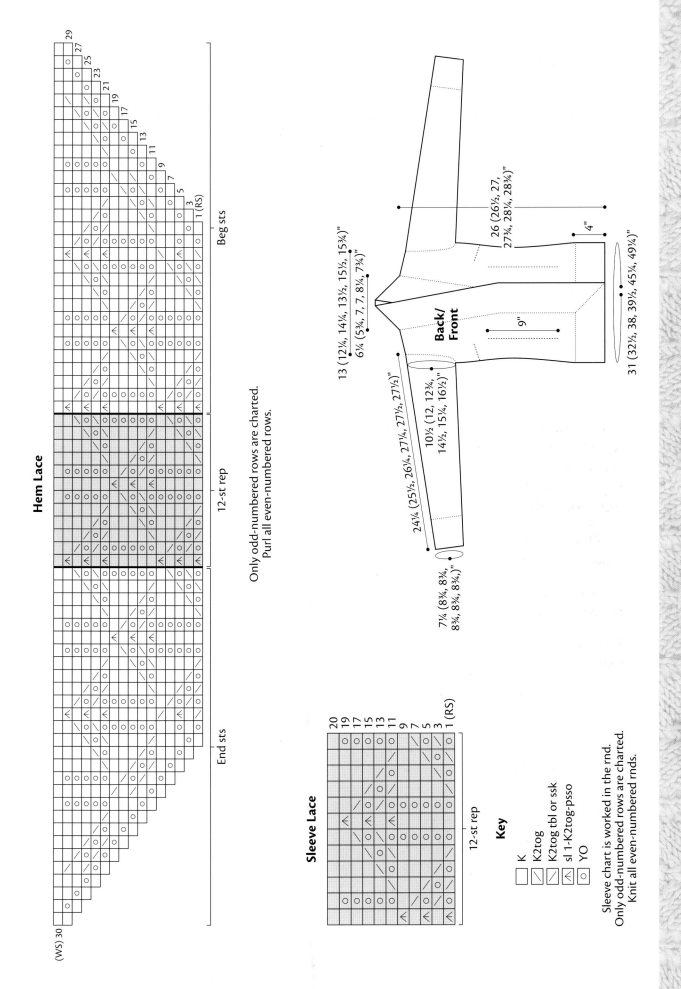

(WS) 30

29
27
25
23
21
19
17
15
13
11
9
7
5
3
1 (RS)

Beg sts

12-st rep

End sts

Only odd-numbered rows are charted.
Purl all even-numbered rows.

**Sleeve Lace**

20
19
17
15
13
11
9
7
5
3
1 (RS)

12-st rep

**Key**

| | K |
| / | K2tog |
| / | K2tog tbl or ssk |
| ⋀ | sl 1-K2tog-psso |
| ○ | YO |

Sleeve chart is worked in the rnd.
Only odd-numbered rows are charted.
Knit all even-numbered rnds.

26 (26½, 27,
27¾, 28¼, 28¾)"

4"

31 (32¼, 38, 39½, 45¼, 49¼)"

**Back/ Front**

9"

13 (12¼, 14¼, 13½, 15½, 15¾)"

6¼ (5¾, 7, 7, 8¼, 7¾)"

10½ (12, 12¾,
14½, 15¼, 16½)"

24¼ (25½, 26¼, 27¼, 27½, 27½)"

7¼ (8¾, 8¾,
8¾, 8¾, 8¾,)"

# Lace Mesh TRIANGULAR SHAWL

### Designed by Evelyn A. Clark

Lace mesh was used for this triangular shawl that's knit from the top down to a scalloped edging. Since the edging can be worked after any 20-row lace-mesh repeat, the size of the shawl can be customized. The sample is knit in lace-weight Shetland, creating a versatile accessory for both day and evening wear. This design could also be knit in fingering, sport, DK, or light worsted-weight yarns, using needles of the appropriate size for the chosen yarn.

**Skill Level:** Intermediate ◼◼◼◻

**Finished Measurements:** 26" deep and 52" across top edge, blocked

## MATERIALS

3 balls of Jamieson & Smith 2-Ply Shetland Lace-weight (100% Shetland wool; 25 g; 185 yds) in color L77 **❶**

Size 4 (3.5 mm) circular needle, 24" long, or size to obtain gauge

3 stitch markers

Tapestry needle

Size F crochet hook and 1 yard smooth waste yarn for provisional cast on

Blocking wires and/or rustproof pins

**Gauge:** 26 sts and 32 rows = 4" in St st

**Pattern Note:** Until scalloped edging, shawl incs 4 sts on EOR, inside the garter st borders, and on each side of the center st. Markers are used after the first 2 border sts, before the center st, and before the last 2 border sts.

## INSTRUCTIONS

Beg at center back neck with garter-st tab. With provisional CO using crochet hook and waste yarn, ch 4. With shawl yarn and knitting needles, knit 2 sts in 2 back loops of chain.

**Rows 1–6:** Knit.

**Row 7:** K2; rotate rectangle to PU 1 st in each of 3 garter st ridges near edge of tab; remove waste yarn from 2 knit sts in ch, place sts on needle and knit them—7 sts.

Beg lace mesh charts.

### Lace Mesh Charts

**Note:** The triangle shawl consists of 2 triangles separated by a center st. Work charts from right to left to center st, for second half, ignore 2 border sts and work chart again from right to left, working 2 border sts at end instead of center st.

Only odd-numbered rows are charted except for the last even-numbered row. Work all even (WS) rows as follows: K2, purl to last 2 sts, K2.

**Chart 1 (lace mesh beg):** Work rows 1–20 of chart once—47 sts.

**Chart 2 (lace mesh rep):** Work rows 1–20 of chart a total of 5 times—247 sts—or to desired length before ending. Be sure to end with row 20.

**Chart 3 (lace mesh ending):** Work rows 1–8 of chart once—263 sts.

**Chart 4 (scalloped edging):** Work rows 1–8 of chart once. St count does not change until row 7, and rep is worked to ending marker, not center marker—315 sts.

**On next RS row:** Work elastic BO as follows: K2, *sl st back to left needle, K2tog tbl, K1, and rep from * until all sts have been BO.

## Finishing

Weave in ends. Wash and block to dimensions by pulling out points along side edges at each "YO, K1tbl YO," and pinning in place.

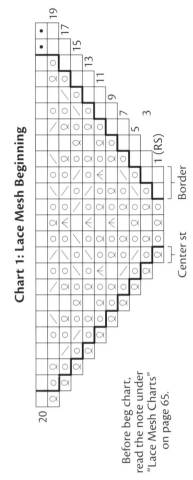

**Chart 1: Lace Mesh Beginning**

Before beg chart, read the note under "Lace Mesh Charts" on page 65.

## Chart 2: Lace Mesh Repeat

Work rows 1–50 five times total, or to desired length before ending, work 10-st rep two additional times every 20 rows.

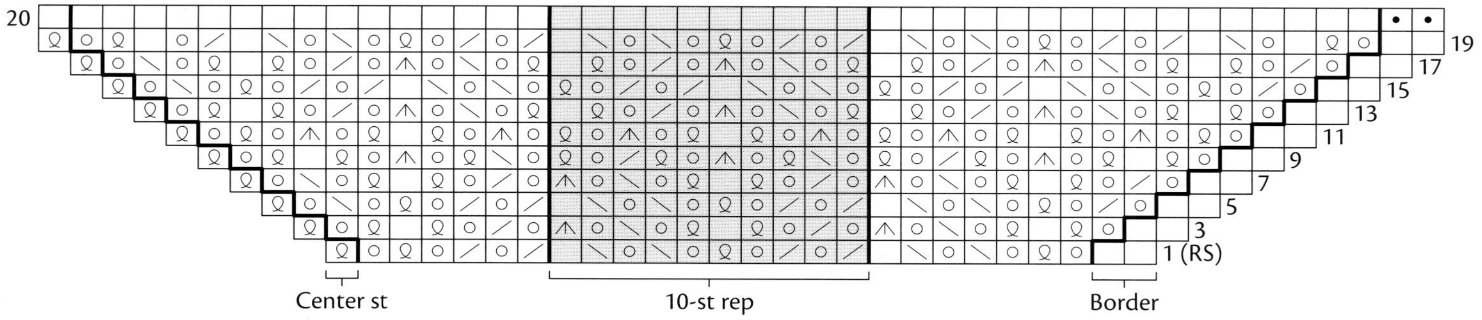

Border

10-st rep

Center st

Center st

## Chart 3: Lace Mesh Ending

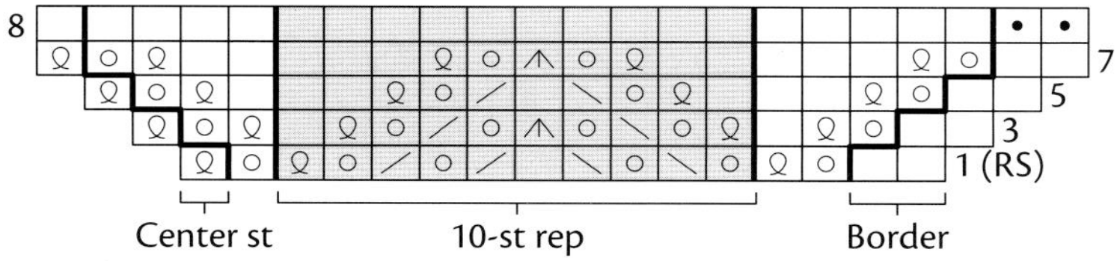

Border

10-st rep

Center st

## Chart 4: Scalloped Edging

Work rep to end border, not center st.

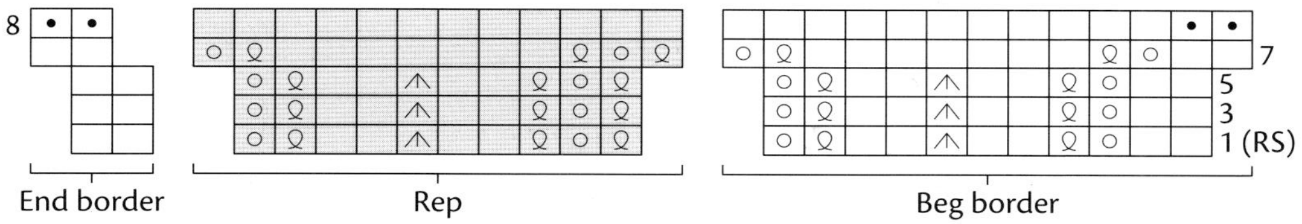

Beg border

Rep

End border

### Key

| | K on RS, P on WS |
| • | K on WS |
| ⚲ | K1 tbl |
| ╲ | K2tog |
| ╱ | K2tog tbl or ssk |
| ⋀ | sl 1-K2tog-psso |
| ○ | YO |

Read charts from bottom to top and from right to left.

Only odd-numbered rows are charted. Work all even-numbered rows as: K2, purl to last 2 sts, K2.

Edging chart 4 is worked to ending border instead of center stitch.

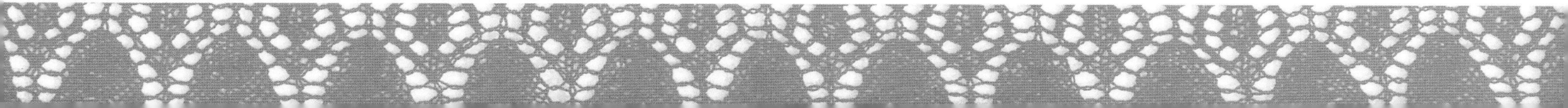

# Ripple and Bead CARDIGAN
## Designed by Sauniell Nicole Connally

This allover lace cardigan gives the stylish look of detailed lace while still providing enough coverage to give a little warmth. Simple shaping and drop-shoulder sleeves give the piece a classic and flattering look without making the pattern too complex. Made with a machine-washable yarn, it is great for any daytime look. Choose a nice deep shade and this cardigan would work great for a night out.

**Skill Level:** Intermediate ◖■■▢

**Size:** S (M, L, XL, 2X)

**Finished Bust:** 38 (40, 45, 48, 54)", including front bands

**Finished Length:** 28 (28½, 29, 29½, 29½)"

## MATERIALS

7 (8, 8, 8, 9) skeins of Gems Light Worsted from Louet (100% merino wool; 100g; 175 yds) in color 80 Terra Cotta ❸

Size 7 (4.5 mm) circular needle, 16" long, or size to obtain gauge

Size 6 (4.0 mm) circular needle, 32" long

4 split ring stitch markers or scrap yarn

5 stitch markers

3 stitch holders or scrap yarn

Tapestry needle

5 buttons, ¾" diameter

Sewing needle and matching thread

**Gauge:** 19 sts and 26 rows = 4" in ripple and bead mesh patt on larger needle

## BACK

With larger needle, CO 97 (102, 114, 118, 134) sts.

Knit 6 rows.

**Setup row (RS):** K1, P2 (4, 2, 3, 2), K1, pm, work row 1 of ripple and bead mesh chart (page 71), pm, K1 (1, 0, 1, 0), P5 (6, 4, 4, 4), K1 (1, 0, 1, 0), pm, work row 1 of chart, pm, K1, P2 (4, 2, 3, 2), K1.

Work patt as established through row 14 on chart.

## Shape Back

**Dec row (RS):** Sl1-K1-psso, work in patt to last 2 sts, K2tog.

Rep dec row every 8th row twice—91 (96, 108, 112, 128) sts.

Work even for 7 rows.

**Dec row (RS):** Work to marker, sl marker, sl1-K1-psso 1 (1, 0, 1, 0) time, P2tog 0 (0, 1, 0, 1) times, work in patt to end.

Rep dec row every 8th row twice—88 (93, 105, 109, 125) sts.

Work even until piece measures 20". End after a WS row.

## Shape Armholes

BO 0 (2, 0, 0, 0) sts at beg of next RS row and following WS row—88 (89, 105, 109, 125) sts. Mark beg of previous 2 rows with split ring markers or scrap yarn to indicate start of armholes. Work even until armholes measure 8 (8½, 9, 9½, 9½)". End with a WS row.

**Next row (RS):** Knit.

Place first 28 (28, 34, 36, 42) sts on holder for shoulder, place 32 (33, 37, 37, 41) sts on holder for neck, place rem sts on holder for other shoulder.

## LEFT FRONT

With larger needle, CO 47 (49, 57, 58, 68) sts. Knit 6 rows.

**Setup row (RS):** K2, P2 (4, 2, 3, 2), pm, work row 1 of chart, pm, K2 (2, 2, 2 3).

Work patt as established through row 14 on chart.

### Side Shaping

**Dec row (RS):** K1, sl1-K1-psso, work to end.

Rep dec row every 8 rows 2 more times—44 (46, 54, 55, 65) sts.

Work even until piece measures 19 (19, 18½, 18½, 18½)".

### Neck and Armhole Shaping

**Dec row (RS):** Work to the last 3 sts, K2tog, K1.

Rep dec row every RS row 15 (17, 19, 18, 23) times.

When piece measures 20", on next RS row, BO 0 (2, 0, 0, 0) sts and mark beg of row with split ring st marker or scrap yarn—28 (26, 34, 36, 41) sts.

Work even until armhole measures same as back. End with a WS row.

**Next row (RS):** Knit.

Place rem sts on holder.

## RIGHT FRONT

With larger needle, CO 47 (49, 57, 58, 68) sts. Knit 6 rows.

**Setup row (RS):** K2 (2, 2, 2, 3), pm, work row 1 of chart, pm, P2 (4, 2, 3, 2), K2.

Work as for left front, with neckline decs at beg of RS rows and armhole decs at beg of WS rows.

## SLEEVES

With larger needles, CO 75 (79, 85, 87, 87) sts.

Knit 4 rows.

**Setup row (RS):** K1, P1 (3, 1, 2, 2), work row 1 of chart, P1 (3, 1, 2, 2), K1.

Work in patts as established until piece measures 19", ending on a RS row.

Knit 3 rows. BO all sts.

## FINISHING

Join shoulders with 3-needle BO. Using split ring markers as a guide, sew sleeves into armholes. Sew side and underarm seams.

**Button band:** With smaller needle, RS facing you, and starting at bottom of right front, PU 26 sts, (pm, PU 16 sts) 4 times, pm, PU 44 (47, 49, 51, 51) sts, knit sts from back neck holder, PU 134 (137, 139, 141, 141) sts down left front—300 (307, 315, 319, 323) sts. Knit 1 row.

**Buttonhole row (RS):** Knit to 2 sts before marker, YO, sl1-K1-psso (buttonhole made); knit, rep buttonhole at each marker, knit to end of row.

Knit 3 rows. BO all sts.

Weave in ends. Wash and block to dimensions.

## Ripple and Bead Mesh

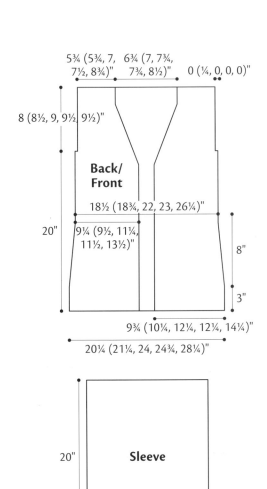

(WS) 36

Row numbers (right side): 35, 33, 31, 29, 27, 25, 23, 21, 19, 17, 15, 13, 11, 9, 7, 5, 3, 1 (RS)

10 end sts     10-st rep     1 beg st

### Key

- ☐ K on RS, P on WS
- Q K1 tbl
- / K2tog
- \ K2tog tbl or ssk
- ⋀ sl 1-K2tog-psso
- ○ YO

Only odd-numbered rows are charted.
Purl all even-numbered rows.

---

**Back/Front**

5¾ (5¾, 7, 7½, 8¾)"   6¾ (7, 7¾, 7¾, 8½)"   0 (¼, 0, 0, 0)"

8 (8½, 9, 9½, 9½)"

18½ (18¾, 22, 23, 26¼)"

20"

9¼ (9½, 11¼, 11½, 13½)"

8"

3"

9¾ (10¼, 12¼, 12¼, 14¼)"

20¼ (21¼, 24, 24¾, 28¼)"

**Sleeve**

20"

15¾ (16½, 17¾, 18¼, 18¼)"

# Filigree Diamonds AFGHAN
## Designed by Deborah Robson

Almost 40 years ago, a friend made designer Deborah an afghan. It's absolutely perfect for naps. She and her daughter both love it, so Deb figured it was past time that they had two. The original was knitted in a horseshoe pattern in bulky acrylic. This is a more complex lace and worked in bulky wool— it succeeds admirably

**Skill Level:** Intermediate ◖■■◻

**Finished Measurements:** 55" x 60 (64)"

## MATERIALS

8 (9) skeins of Burly Spun from Brown Sheep Company (100% wool; 8 oz; 130 yds) in color BX181 Prairie Fire

Size 13 (9 mm) circular needle, 40" long, or size to obtain gauge

Stitch markers (optional but strongly suggested)

**Gauge**

10 sts and 13 rows = 4" in St st unblocked

10¾ sts and 13 rows = 4" in lace patt unblocked

Blocked gauge: Approx 9 sts and 12 rows = 4" in lace patt

## AFGHAN

CO 125 sts.

## BEGINNING BORDER

**Row 1 (WS):** *K1, P1; rep from * to last st, K1.

**Row 2:** Knit.

**Row 3:** K1, P1, knit to last 2 sts, P1, K1.

**Rows 4 and 6:** K2, P1, knit to last 3 sts, P1, K2.

**Rows 5 and 7:** K1, P1, K1, purl to last 3 sts, K1, P1, K1.

## Central Pattern

*When adding new balls of yarn, splice within St st part of a border.*

Work setup rows of filigree diamond chart (page 75). If desired, pm between lace patt reps; sm as necessary to accommodate decs between reps on rows 5, 13, and 25.

Work rows 1–28 of chart until 6 (6½) reps are completed (if working 6½ reps, work an extra set of rows 1–14 before final border).

## Final Border

**Row 1 (RS):** K2, P1, knit to last 3 sts, P1, K2.

**Row 2:** K1, P1, K1, purl to last 3 sts, K1, P1, K1.

**Row 3:** K2, P1, knit to last 3 sts, P1, K2.

**Row 4:** K1, P1, knit to last 2 sts, P1, K1.

**Row 5:** Knit.

**Row 6:** *K1, P1; rep from * to last st, K1.

BO all sts pw.

## FINISHING

Weave in ends. Block to dimensions.

**Filigree Diamond**

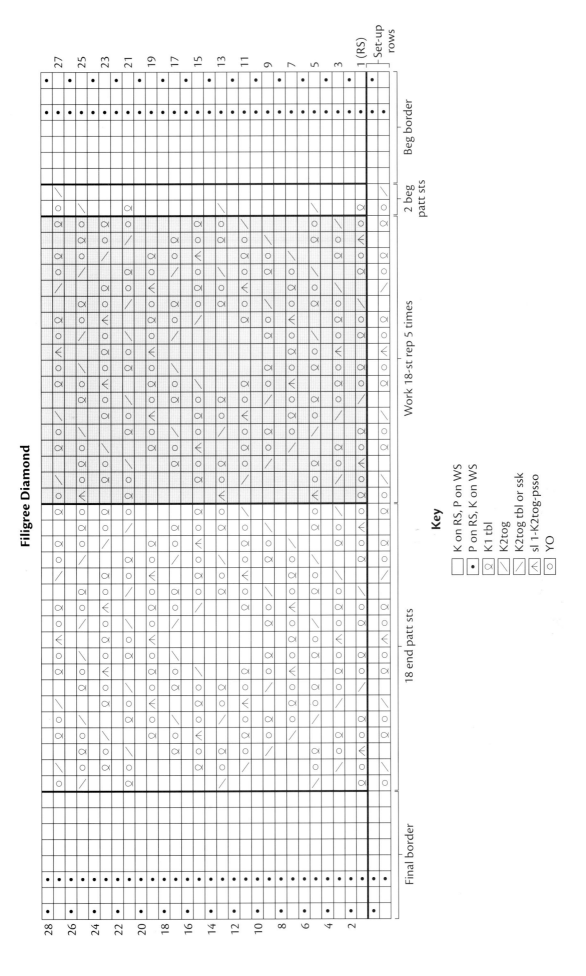

**Key**

| | K on RS, P on WS |
| --- | --- |
| • | P on RS, K on WS |
| ⋈ | K1 tbl |
| \ | K2tog |
| / | K2tog tbl or ssk |
| ⋏ | sl 1-K2tog-psso |
| ○ | YO |

# Trellis and Flowers STOLE
## Designed by Alice Scherp

This stole features a garden theme, with the trellis pattern on the outside edge and diamond ladders framing the floral mesh pattern in the center. The different colors separate the patterns. This handspun lace-weight qiviut yarn has a lovely transparent look. Working with color changes was a bit of a challenge, but the results are well worth the effort!

**Skill Level:** Experienced ◼◼◼◼

**Finished Measurements:** 24" x 84", blocked

## MATERIALS

Handspun 2-ply yarn* (80% qiviut, 10% silk, 10% merino; 2.6 oz total; approx 600 yds) in the following amounts and colors: (0)

A  .65 oz; approx 150 yds in natural

B  1.95 oz; approx 450 yds in hand-dyed heather

Size 4 (3.5 mm) circular needle, 24" long, or size to obtain gauge

Blocking wires and/or rustproof pins

Tapestry needle

*The designer spun her own yarn for this stole. Any ultra-fine, lace-weight qiviut, cashmere, or alpaca would make a beautiful stole.

**Gauge:** 32 sts and 36 rows = 4" in floral mesh patt

## PATTERN STITCH

**Seed Stitch**

(Worked over an odd number of sts)

**Row 1 (RS):** K1, (P1, K1) to end of row.

**Row 2:** Purl the knit sts and knit the purl sts as they face you.

Rep row 2 for patt.

## INSTRUCTIONS

Use a separate ball of yarn for each color area. To change colors in middle of a row: With the first color, knit up to color change, then drop first color, pick up second color, crossing yarn underneath first color, and work first st tightly. Give end of old color a slight tug to lock colors tog, then cont knitting with second color.

With A, CO 163 sts.

### Seed Stitch Edging

Work seed stitch for 1", ending after a WS row.

### Trellis Pattern

**Next row (RS):** With A, work 8 sts in seed st; with B, work row 1 of trellis chart (page 79); with A, work 8 sts in seed st.

Work patts as established, working rows 1–34 of Trellis chart once, then rows 3–34 once more; total of 66 rows of trellis patt.

### Diamond Ladders Pattern

**Next row (RS):** With A, work 8 sts in seed st; with B, cont trellis chart; with A, work row 1 of diamond ladders chart (page 79) over next 17 sts; work 43 sts in St st; work row 1 of diamond ladders chart over next 17 sts; with B, cont trellis chart; with A, work 8 sts in seed st.

Work patts as established until rows 1–10 of diamond ladders chart have been worked once.

## Floral Mesh Pattern

**Next row (RS):** Work in colors and patts as established to end of first diamond ladders chart, with B, K1, work row 1 of floral mesh chart, K1, cont in colors and patts as established to end of row.

Work patts as established until 45 vertical reps of diamond ladders with floral mesh in the center are complete.

## Reverse Patterning for Second End

Work diamond ladders patt, then trellis patt, then seed stitch edging.

BO all sts loosely.

## FINISHING

Wash and block to dimensions. If desired, when dry lightly steam edges and corners.

## Floral Mesh

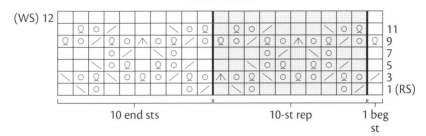

(WS) 12

11
9
7
5
3
1 (RS)

10 end sts · 10-st rep · 1 beg st

## Trellis

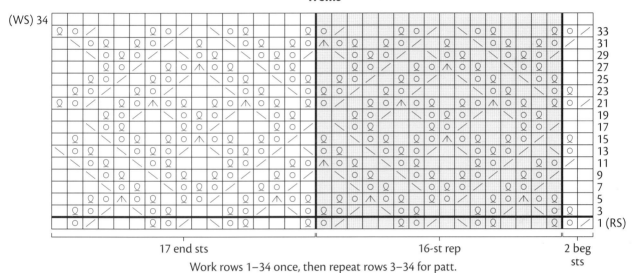

(WS) 34

33
31
29
27
25
23
21
19
17
15
13
11
9
7
5
3
1 (RS)

17 end sts · 16-st rep · 2 beg sts

Work rows 1–34 once, then repeat rows 3–34 for patt.

## Diamond Ladders

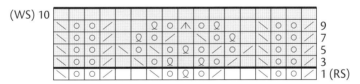

(WS) 10

9
7
5
3
1 (RS)

Worked over 17 sts.
Work rows 1 and 2 once;
rep rows 3–10 for vertical rep.

## Key

| | |
|---|---|
| ☐ | K on RS, P on WS |
| Ọ | K1 tbl |
| ∕ | K2tog |
| ∖ | K2tog tbl or ssk |
| ⋀ | sl 1-K2tog-psso |
| ○ | YO |

Only odd-numbered rows are charted.
Purl all even-numbered rows.

# Cherry Tree Hill Folk SHAWL
## *Designed by Cheryl Potter*

 This folk shawl will remind you of pioneer women traveling west in wagons. Each lace medallion is knit in a different hand-dyed solid or colorway panel running up the center of the shawl accented by coordinating fringe. The yarn is easy-knit and easy-care superwash merino.

**Skill Level:** Intermediate ●■■◻

**Finished Measurements:** 43" long x 77" wide

## MATERIALS

Supersock DK from Cherry Tree Hill Yarns (100% superwash merino; 4 oz; 360 yds) in the following amounts and colors: **3**

- A   1 skein Slate
- B   1 skein Misty Moor
- C   2 skeins Loden
- D   2 skeins Peacock
- E   2 skeins Purple

Size 7 (4.5 mm) circular needle, 29" long, or size to obtain gauge

2 stitch markers

Size H crochet hook (optional for fringe)

**Gauge:** 21 sts and 30 rows = 4" over St st

## INSTRUCTIONS

With color A, CO 3 sts.

**Row 1 (RS):** K1, YO, knit to last st, YO, K1.

**Row 2 (WS):** Purl.

Cont working in St st and inc 1 st each side every RS row to 35 sts. Beg chart (page 83), centering sts as follows:

**Next row (RS):** K1, YO, K1, pm, work row 1 of scroll chart over next 31 sts, pm, K1, YO, K1.

Work all rows of chart between markers while cont to inc at beg and end of every RS row for entire shawl.

Work 4 rows in St st.

With B, *work 4 rows in St st. Work all rows of chart between markers. Work 4 rows in St st. Rep from * with C, then with D, then with E.

BO all sts loosely.

## FINISHING

Weave in ends. Block to dimensions.

**Fringe (optional):** Cut enough 10"-long pieces of yarn from A, B, C, D, and E for fringe around the edge of the shawl. Match fringe color to corresponding section color and place fringes in every other row along diagonal edges. Using one strand of yarn, fold fringe in half, insert crochet hook into st at edge from front to back. Catch folded fringe and pull through knitted piece, creating a loop, and then catch and pull the fringe strands through the loop and pull tight.

## Scroll

(WS) 56

55
53
51
49
47
45
43
41
39
37
35
33
31
29
27
25
23
21
19
17
15
13
11
9
7
5
3
1 (RS)

Worked over 31 sts

## Key

| | |
|---|---|
| ☐ | K on RS, P on WS |
| ℚ | K1 tbl |
| ╱ | K2tog |
| ╲ | K2tog tbl or ssk |
| ⋀ | sl 1-K2tog-psso |
| ○ | YO |

Only odd-numbered rows are charted.
Purl all even-numbered rows.

# Copper Queen Beaded STOLE
*Designed by Renee Leverington*

This versatile stole makes a great wrap for cool summer evenings or a warm scarf for chilly fall days. The beaded accents make it a great accessory for your favorite jeans or your little black dress!

**Skill Level:** Intermediate ■■■□

**Finished Measurements:** 21" wide x 85" long

## MATERIALS

6 skeins of Jamieson & Smith 2-Ply Jumper-weight (100% Shetland wool; 25g; 125 yds) in color FC38 Copper

Size 6 (4 mm) circular needle, 24" long, or size to obtain gauge

5 stitch markers

10 opaque green bicone beads, 4 mm

15 grams of copper glass seed beads

Steel crochet hook small enough to fit through hole in bicone beads

Transparent (or color to match yarn) bead thread

Beading needle

Tapestry needle

Blocking wires and/or rustproof pins

**Gauge:** 4½ sts and 6 rows = 4" over St st

## SPECIAL TECHNIQUES

**Knitted Cast On:** Make a sl knot with a 3" to 4" tail and place on left needle. K1, leaving first st on needle, then turn right needle toward you and place new st on left needle. Cont in this manner until the desired number of sts are cast on.

**Attaching bicone beads:** Place a bicone bead on the hook end of the crochet hook, insert crochet hook into the st that the bead is to be attached to, and remove the st from the left needle, slide bead down onto the st, then place the st back onto the left needle. Knit that st as usual. The seed beads will be sewn on after you have blocked the shawl.

## INSTRUCTIONS

CO 61 sts, using knitted CO method, create edge picot as follows: CO 5 sts then BO 3 sts as follows: K1, (K1tbl, pass the first knitted st over second st) twice, place rem st on right-hand needle back on left-hand needle. Cont adding sts by CO 5 sts and BO 3 sts, until you have 61 sts and 20 picots on your needle.

Work all rows in chart A (page 86) once.

Work all rows in chart B (page 87) a total of 8 times.

Work all rows in chart C (page 87) once.

## FINISHING

**Binding off:** Using knitted CO method, create edge picot as follows: *CO 3 sts then BO 3 sts as follows: K1, (K1tbl, pass first knitted st over second st) twice, (K1, return both sts to left needle and K2tog tbl, K1) 3 times, place rem st on right-hand needle back on left-hand needle. Rep from * until all sts have been bound off, you should have 20 picots on BO edge.

Weave in ends. Wash and block to dimensions.

**Beading:** Sew on seed beads using beading thread and needle. Cut a length of thread approx 2 times the width of blocked shawl. Attach one end of the thread to bottom corner edge of shawl. Thread about an inch of beads on needle, then run needle through first picot, making sure to prevent thread from showing through front of st. Cont adding beads in this manner until you reach other corner; secure thread by knotting and weaving in ends, making sure thread does not show through front of work. Rep on opposite edge of shawl.

## Chart A

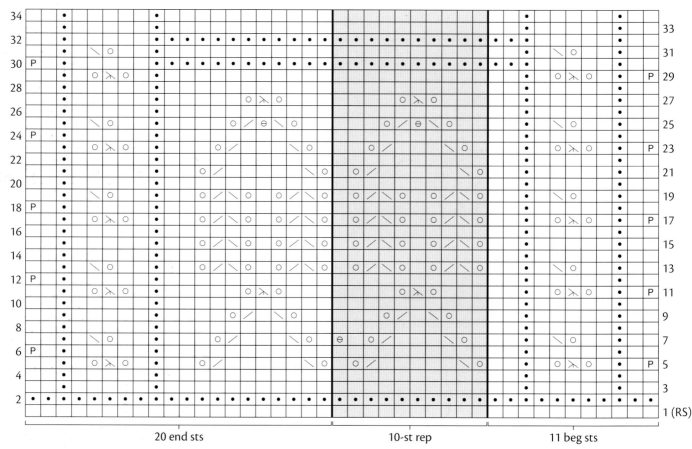

20 end sts          10-st rep          11 beg sts

### Key

| | |
|---|---|
| ☐ | K on RS, P on WS |
| • | P on RS, K on WS |
| ℚ | K1 tbl |
| ╱ | K2tog |
| ╲ | K2tog tbl or ssk |
| ⋏ | sl 2-K1-p2sso |
| ○ | YO |
| ⊖ | Bead placement: See "Attaching Bicone Beads" on page 85. |
| P | Edge picot: Using the knitted cast on method above, CO 2 sts then BO 2 sts as follows: K1, (K1 tbl, pass first knitted st over the second st) twice. You will have 1 st rem on right needle. Work rem sts as charted. |

## Chart B

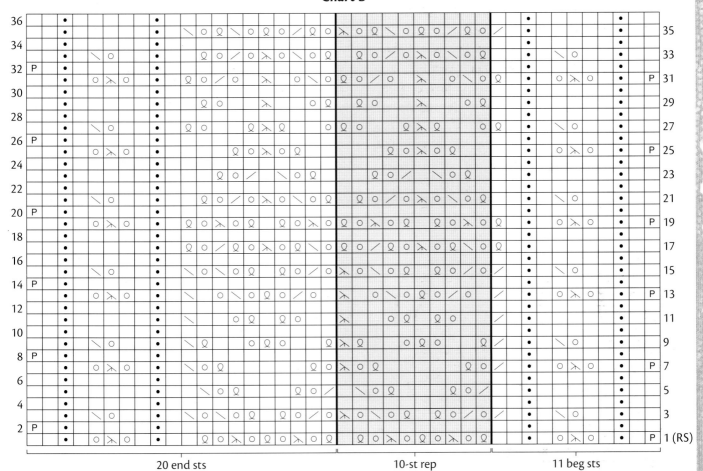

20 end sts     10-st rep     11 beg sts

## Chart C

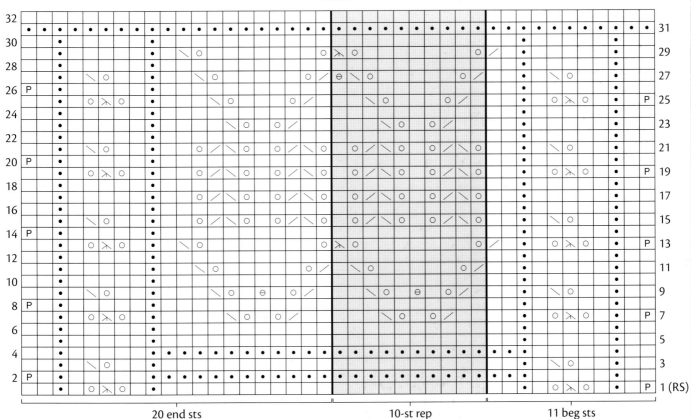

20 end sts     10-st rep     11 beg sts

# Lace and Colorwork Wimple

*Designed by Annie Modesitt*

This romantic hood uses a floral lace motif that is echoed in colorwork. It's a wonderful, warm design that will keep your head and neck toasty even in the coldest weather, and all without ruining your hairstyle.

**Skill Level:** Experienced ◼◼◼◻

**Finished Measurements:** 30" circumference and 22" long

## MATERIALS

Silk Rhapsody from Artyarns (100% silk wound with 70% kid mohair and 30% silk; 100 g; 260 yds) in the following amounts and colors:

- A  1 ball of color 113 Browns

- B  2 balls of color 255 Cool Light Green

- C  1 ball of color 135 Warm Reds

- D  1 ball of Silk Mohair from Artyarns (70% kid mohair, 30% silk; 230 yds; 25 g) in color MS417 Warm Beige

Size 8 (5 mm) circular needle, 36" long, or size to obtain gauge for colorwork

Size 7 (4.5 mm) circular needle, 36" long, or size to obtain gauge for lace

Stitch marker

Tapestry needle

### Gauge

20 sts and 24 rows = 4" in floral colorwork patt on larger needles with colors A, B, and C

One lace panel rep = 3" in floral lace patt on size 7 needles with color D

## BOTTOM HEM

With smaller needles and A, CO 160 sts. Work in St st for 4 rows, join work, pm to note start of rnd. Work 5 rnds St st.

### Begin Twisted Float Trim

Turn work so you're working on WS. Keeping strands to RS of work and knitting or purling into back of st to twist it, work 1 rnd as follows: K1 with B, K1 with A, drop strand, *bring strand of B over strand of A, K1 with B, bring strand of A over strand of B, K1 with A; rep from * to last st, K1 with B. Notice that this will twist the strands of yarn. Untwist yarns before proceeding.

### Begin Bottom Colorwork

Turn work so RS is facing. With larger needles and starting with row 1 of floral colorwork chart (page 91), rep all rows of chart twice.

Next rnd: With A, purl.

Next rnd: With D, knit.

Next rnd: With A, purl.

## BEGIN LACE SECTION

Using smaller needles and starting with row 1 of lace chart (page 91), change to D and work through row 36 of chart, then start with row 1 and work through row 22—58 rows total.

## BEGIN TOP COLORWORK

Change to larger needles.

**Next rnd:** With A, purl.

**Next rnd:** With D, knit.

**Next rnd:** With A, purl.

Turn colorwork chart over so that row 1 is on the top and row 36 is on the bottom.

Starting at row 36, beg colorwork chart using colors as designated.

Work all rows of chart twice, ending with row 1. BO very loosely.

## FINISHING

Weave in ends. Wash and block to dimensions. Turn bottom hem up so that edge folds at twisted float trim and whipstitch facing to WS of wimple. Fold top colorwork in half to the inside and whipstitch to WS of wimple so that WS will not show around face when worn.

**Lace**

16-st rep

1 beg st

Row numbers: 36 35 34 33 32 31 30 29 28 27 26 25 24 23 22 21 20 19 18 17 16 15 14 13 12 11 10 9 8 7 6 5 4 3 2 1

**Key**

- ☐ K on RS, P on WS
- Ⓠ K1 tbl
- ╲ K2tog
- ╱ K2tog tbl or ssk
- ⟨ sl 1-K2tog-psso
- ○ YO

All rnds of charts are worked from right to left.

**Floral Colorwork**

Row numbers: 36 35 34 33 32 31 30 29 28 27 26 25 24 23 22 21 20 19 18 17 16 15 14 13 12 11 10 9 8 7 6 5 4 3 2 1

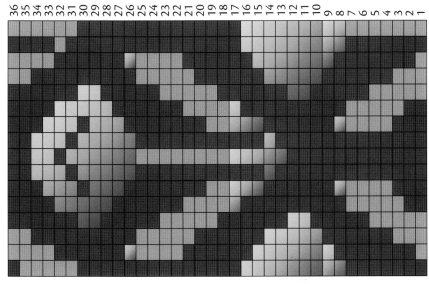

**Key**

- ■ A (113 Browns)
- ■ B (224 Cool Light Green)
- ■ C (135 Warm Reds)

Work rnds 1–7 with A and B.
Work rnds 8–17 with A and C.
Work rnds 18–25 with A and B.
Work rnds 26–30 with A and C.
Work rnds 31–34 with A, B, and C.
Work rnds 35 and 36 with A and B.

# Revelry in Bloom Top
### Designed by L'Tanya Durante

The lace at the hemline and yoke mimics the detailed embroidery of the traditional Indian tunic. A diagonal eyelet pattern throughout the body adds interest and a little eye candy. This versatile tunic can be worn alone or over a tank top. As the lace reveals its pattern, you won't have a dull moment knitting this project.

**Skill Level:** Intermediate ■■■◻

**Size:** S (M, L, XL)

**Finished Bust:** 40 (42½, 46½, 51)"

**Finished Length:** 26¼ (26¾, 28¼, 30¼)"

## MATERIALS

4 (5, 6, 6) Mini-cones of Maine Line 2/8 Worsted Wool from JaggerSpun (100% wool; 275 yds) in color Marigold

Size 5 (3.75 mm) needles, or size to obtain gauge

Size 5 (3.75 mm) circular needle, 29" long

7 (8, 10, 11) stitch markers: 4 (4, 5, 6) in color A and 3 (4, 5, 5) in color B

Tapestry needle

**Gauge:** 26 sts and 29 rows = 4" in St st

## BACK

CO 138 (144, 155, 169) sts.

**Next row (WS):** Knit

**Next row (RS):** K7 (10, 0, 7), *work row 1 of 31-st rep on floral panel (page 97) 4 (4, 5, 5) times, K7 (10, 0, 7).

Work next 35 rows, keeping 7 (10, 0, 7) sts at beg and end in St st and 31-st rep as established, ending with row 36.

**Next row (RS):** Work 4 rows even.

**Dec row (RS):** K2tog, knit to last 2 sts, ssk—136 (142, 153, 167) sts.

**Next row (WS):** Work 5 rows even.

## Shape Waist

**Dec row (RS):** Work dec and AT SAME TIME beg eyelet pattern as follows: K2tog, K13 (13, 11, 8), *pm-A, work row 1 of eyelet chart (page 97), K13, rep from * 4 (4, 5, 6) times, work row 1 of eyelet chart once more, K12 (18, 11, 8), ssk—134 (140, 151, 165) sts.

**Next 5 rows:** Work next 5 rows of eyelet patt, working in St st between eyelets.

**Dec row (RS):** K2tog, knit to last 2 sts, ssk—132 (138, 149, 163) sts.

**Next 5 rows:** Work even.

**Dec row (RS):** K2tog, knit to last 2 sts, ssk—130 (136, 147, 161) sts.

**Next 5 rows:** Work even.

**Dec row (RS):** Work dec and AT SAME TIME beg alternating eyelet patt as follows: K2tog, K21 (21, 1, 18), *pm-B, work row 1 of eyelet patt, K13, rep from * 3 (4, 5, 5) times, work row 1 of eyelet patt once more, K18 (4, 15, 12), ssk—128 (134, 145, 159) sts.

Work dec on every 6th row 4 (3, 3, 2) times and AT SAME TIME working eyelet patt with alternating placement—120 (128, 139, 155) sts.

Work even in established patt until back measures 11 (11½, 12½, 13½)". End after a WS row.

Inc row (RS): Inc 1 st at beg and end of this row and then on every 8th row 5 (5, 6, 6) times—130 (138, 151, 167) sts.

Cont in established patt until back measures 18 (18½, 19¼, 19½)".

## Shape Armholes

BO 6 (6, 7, 8) sts at beg of next 2 rows; then BO 4 sts at beg of next 2 rows; then dec 1 st at beg and end of next RS row 6 (7, 9, 9) times—98 (104, 111, 125) sts rem.

Work even in alternating eyelet patt as established until piece measures 25½, (26, 27½, 28½)". End after a WS row.

## Shape Shoulder and Neck

BO 5 sts at beg of next 4 rows—78 (84, 91, 105) sts rem.

Next row (RS): K20 (23, 25, 32), attach a second ball of yarn and BO 38 (38, 41, 41) center sts, finish row—20 (23, 25, 32) sts rem for each shoulder. Beg working shoulders separately.

Right Shoulder: Work 1 row even, then BO 5 sts at beg of row, knit to last 2 sts, K2tog at neck edge on every RS row 2 (2, 2, 3) times—8 (11, 13, 14) sts rem. BO.

Rep for left shoulder, reversing shaping.

## FRONT

Work same as back until front measures 16 (16½, 17, 18)". End after a WS row—130 (138, 151, 167) sts.

## Lace Yoke

Note: Alternating eyelet patt AND center yoke lace patt AND decs (same as back) are worked AT THE SAME TIME.

Next row (RS): Work 43 (47, 46, 54) in established patt, pm, work row 1 of floral panel over center 45 (45, 59, 59) sts, pm, work rem sts in established patt.

## Shape Armholes

When front measures 18 (18½, 19¼, 19½)", work armhole same as back—98 (104, 111, 125) sts.

## Shape Neck and Shoulder

Cont in patt until front measures 24½ (25, 26½, 27¼)". End after a WS row.

Next row (RS): Cont in established patt and using separate balls of yarn, work 39 (42, 42, 49) sts, BO center 20 (20, 27, 27) sts, finish row—39 (42, 42, 49) sts rem for each shoulder. Beg working shoulders separately.

Left shoulder: BO 5 sts at beg of next row for neckline, cont in patt to end—34 (37, 37, 44) sts rem.

Next row (RS): Work in patt to last 2 sts, K2tog at neck edge.

Cont to dec 1 st at neck edge every RS row 10 (10, 8, 9) more times—23 (26, 28, 34) sts rem. When front measures same as back to shoulder, end after a WS row. BO 5 sts at beg of next 3 (3, 3, 4) RS rows—8 (11, 13, 14) sts rem. BO.

Rep for right shoulder, reversing shaping instructions.

## SLEEVES

CO 78 (92, 106, 120) sts.

Work in St until the sleeve measures ½". End after a WS row.

Next row (RS): Inc 1 st at beg and end of this row and on following 8th row—82 (96, 110, 124) sts.

Work 7 rows even.

Next row (eyelet row on RS): K37 (44, 51, 58), pm, beg eyelet patt, K38 (45, 52, 59).

Work 1 (WS) row even.

Inc 1 st at beg and end of every 8th row 6 more times)—94 (108, 122, 136) sts. AT SAME TIME, cont to work 6 rows of eyelet chart one time—1 eyelet made. Work even in St st until the sleeve measures 9" or desired length to underarm.

Shape Cap: BO 6 (6 7, 8) sts at beg of next 4 rows, then BO 4 sts at beg of next 2 rows—74 (88, 100, 112) sts rem. Dec 1 st at beg and end of next RS row 7 (8, 11, 9) times, then dec every 4 rows 4 (4, 3, 4) times, then dec every RS row 1 (2, 2, 0) times, then BO 2 sts at beg of next 4 (2, 2, 18) rows, then BO 3 sts at beg of next 4 (8, 8, 0) rows—18 (20, 26, 34) sts rem. BO.

## FINISHING

Weave in ends. Block front, back, and sleeve pieces to dimensions. Sew shoulder seams. Sew sleeves into armholes. Sew side and underarm seams. Press seams lightly.

Neck edging: Starting at back of neck, PU sts evenly around neckline, picking up approx 1 st for every st across base of front and back neck and 3 sts for every 4 rows on sides of neck. Work applied I-cord as follows: CO 3 sts, *K2, sl next st kw (from CO 3 or 3 sl sts), sl next st kw (from picked-up sts), knit 2 slipped sts tog-tbl, sl 3 sts just knit back onto left needle and rep from * until all sts that were picked up have been worked. Sew both ends of I-cord tog.

Sleeve edging: Starting at underarm seam, PU 1 st in each CO st around cuff. Work applied I-cord as for neck edging.

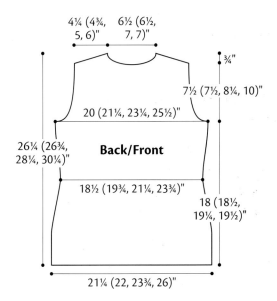

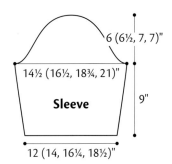

## Floral Panel

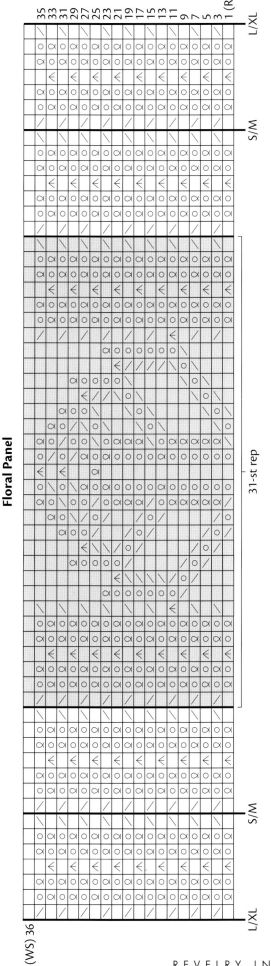

(WS) 36

35
33
31
29
27
25
23
21
19
17
15
13
11
9
7
5
3
1 (RS)

L/XL

S/M

L/XL

S/M

L/XL

31-st rep

For hem, work 31-st rep 4 (4, 5, 5) times.
For yoke, work across rows as indicated for your size.

### Eyelet

6

5
3
1 (RS)

Worked over 7 sts

### Key

☐ K on RS, P on WS
Ⓠ K1 tbl
╱ K2tog
╱ K2tog tbl or ssk
⊼ sl 1-K2tog-psso
○ YO

Only odd-numbered rows are charted.
Purl all even-numbered rows.

# Day and Night: TODDLER CARDIGAN and BLANKET
*Designed by Debbie O'Neill*

This swingy lace cardigan is the perfect addition to any little girl's wardrobe for playtime or special occasions, and it knits up in no time at all. The lacy blanket is both lightweight and cozy. Because it is knit with a machine-washable yarn, your little one can take this blanket everywhere!

## CARDIGAN

**Skill Level:** Intermediate ◼◼◼◻

**Size:** Child's 2 (8)

**Finished Chest:** 22 (28)", including trim

**Finished Length:** 12¾ (14¾)"

## MATERIALS

3 (3) skeins of Shepherd Sport from Lorna's Laces (100% Superwash wool; 2.6 oz; 200 yds) in color Lilac

Size 4 (3.5 mm) needles, or size to obtain gauge

Size 3 (3.25mm) circular needles, 24" long

4 stitch holders

Tapestry needle

3 buttons, ⅝" diameter

Sewing needle and matching thread

**Gauge:** 26 sts and 32 rows = 4" in St st on larger needles

## BACK

With larger needles, CO 67 (89) sts.

**Rows 1–3:** Work in garter st.

**Next row (RS):** Beg row 1 of closed-bud lace chart (page 102), working 22-st rep 2 (3 times).

Work rows 1–36 of chart once, then work rows 11–36 once more.

**Next row (RS):** Cont working even in St st until piece measures 12¾ (14¾)". End on WS row.

**Next row (RS):** K22 (30), BO 23 (29), knit to end of row.

Place shoulder sts on st holders.

## RIGHT FRONT

With larger needles, CO 34 (45) sts.

**Rows 1–3:** Work in garter st.

**Next row (RS):** Beg row 1 of closed-bud lace chart. For Child's 2, start chart on st 12 (working K2tog in place of double dec on row 25) and end on last st of chart. For Child's 8, work across all sts in chart.

Work rows 1–36 of chart once, then work rows 11–36 once more.

**Next row (RS):** Beg St st and work until piece measures 9 (10¼)". End after a WS row.

**Shape Neck:** Work neck shaping as follows:

**Next row (RS):** BO 5 (9) sts at beg of row (neck edge).

**Next row (and all WS rows):** Work even.

**Next row (RS):** BO 3 (3) sts at beg of row (neck edge).

Next RS row: BO 2 (2) sts at beg of row (neck edge).

Next RS row: BO 2 (1) st at beg of row (neck edge)—22 (30) sts rem.

Work even in St st until the right front measures the same as the back. Put rem sts on a st holder.

## LEFT FRONT

Work as for right front, reversing shaping, and starting chart for Child's 2 on first st and ending on 34th st (working K2tog in place of double dec on row 25).

## SLEEVES

*The sleeves are worked in St st with closed-bud lace chart worked over center 23 sts.*

With larger needles, CO 31 (35) sts.

Rows 1–3: Work in garter st.

Next row (RS): K4 (6), pm, work row 1 of closed-bud lace chart for sleeve (page 102), pm, K4 (6). Cont in established patt, working rows 1–36 of chart once, then rep rows 11–36 of chart for length of sleeve. AT SAME TIME, when sleeve measures approx 1", work inc row on next RS row and every 4th row 12 times as follows: K1, M1, work to last st, M1, K1—55 (59) sts.

Cont in patt until sleeve measures 9 (10)".

BO all sts loosely.

## FINISHING

With RS tog, join shoulders using 3-needle BO. Sew sleeves to body. Sew side seams and underarm seams.

Trim: Starting at bottom of right front, using circular small needle, PU approx 6 sts per inch evenly along right front, around neck opening, and down left front. The exact number of sts is not important—you want to pick up a number that works out close to st gauge (approx 200 to 210 sts total). Work 1 row of garter st. On next row (RS), cont to work garter

st, but work 3 buttonholes (K2tog, YO) 2" apart at top of left front. Work 2 more rows of garter st. BO all sts on WS row.

Weave in ends. Block to dimensions.

## BLANKET

Skill Level: Experienced ◀■■▶

Finished Dimensions: Approx 40" x 40" (depending on blocking)

## MATERIALS

7 skeins of Shepherd Sport from Lorna's Laces (100% Superwash wool; 2.6 oz; 200 yds) in color Lilac 🧶3

Size 4 (3.5 mm) set of 5 double-pointed needles, 24"-long and 47"-long circular needles or size to obtain gauge

4 stitch markers

Tapestry needle

Gauge: 20 sts and 28 rows = 4" in St st

### BLANKET NOTES

This blanket is made up of four triangular sections knit in the round from the center. Increases are worked on every other round at the beginning and end of each section.

The first several rounds are charted to show how to establish the pattern. It's assumed that the knitter can determine how to knit the remaining rounds from the instructions that follow.

Each triangular section has a single closed-bud motif worked twice vertically (shown in chart), three closed-bud motifs worked twice vertically (shown in chart once), and five closed-bud motifs worked twice vertically (not shown in chart). The closed-bud motifs are surrounded by stockinette stitches and framed by increases defining each section.

## INSTRUCTIONS

Using dpns, CO 12 sts. Divide sts evenly onto 4 needles. Join to work in the rnd, being careful not to twist sts. Work 1 rnd even.

Beg chart on page 103 to establish patt, changing to circular needles as needed. When working on circular needles, pm between each triangular section to mark where incs should occur.

**Border:** When all closed-bud motifs are worked (195 sts in each triangular section), work 6 rnds of St st, inc as established on odd-numbered rows.

Work 12 rnds of garter st, inc as established on odd-numbered rows—213 sts in each triangular section. BO all sts loosely.

## FINISHING

Weave in ends. Block to dimensions.

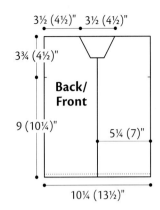

3½ (4½)"  3½ (4½)"

3¾ (4½)"

**Back/ Front**

9 (10¼)"

5¼ (7)"

10¼ (13½)"

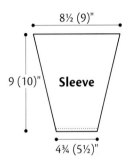

8½ (9)"

9 (10)"  **Sleeve**

4¾ (5½)"

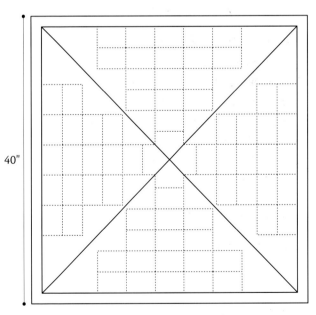

40"

## Closed-Bud Lace for Cardigan

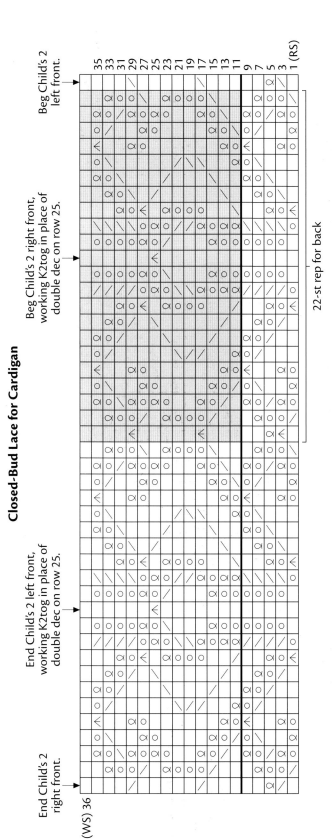

Beg Child's 2 left front.

Beg Child's 2 right front, working K2tog in place of double dec on row 25.

End Child's 2 left front, working K2tog in place of double dec on row 25.

End Child's 2 right front.

35 33 31 29 27 25 23 21 19 17 15 13 11 9 7 5 3 1 (RS)

(WS) 36

22-st rep for back

For back, work across all sts, working 2 (3) reps.
For Child's 2 left and right fronts, works sts as indicated.
For Child's 8 left and right fronts, work across all sts.

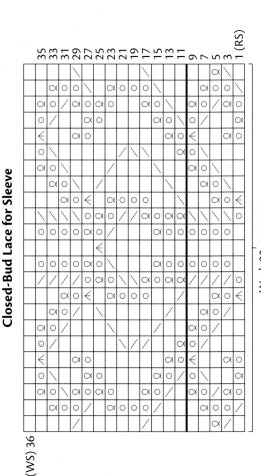

**Key**

| | K on RS, P on WS |
| Ω | K1 tbl |
| \ | K2tog |
| / | K2 tog tbl or ssk |
| ⋏ | sl 1-K2tog-psso |
| o | YO |

Only odd-numbered rows are charted.
Purl all even-numbered rows.

## Closed-Bud Lace for Sleeve

35 33 31 29 27 25 23 21 19 17 15 13 11 9 7 5 3 1 (RS)

(WS) 36

Work 23 sts once.

Work rows 1–36 once, then rep rows 11–36 for length of sleeve.

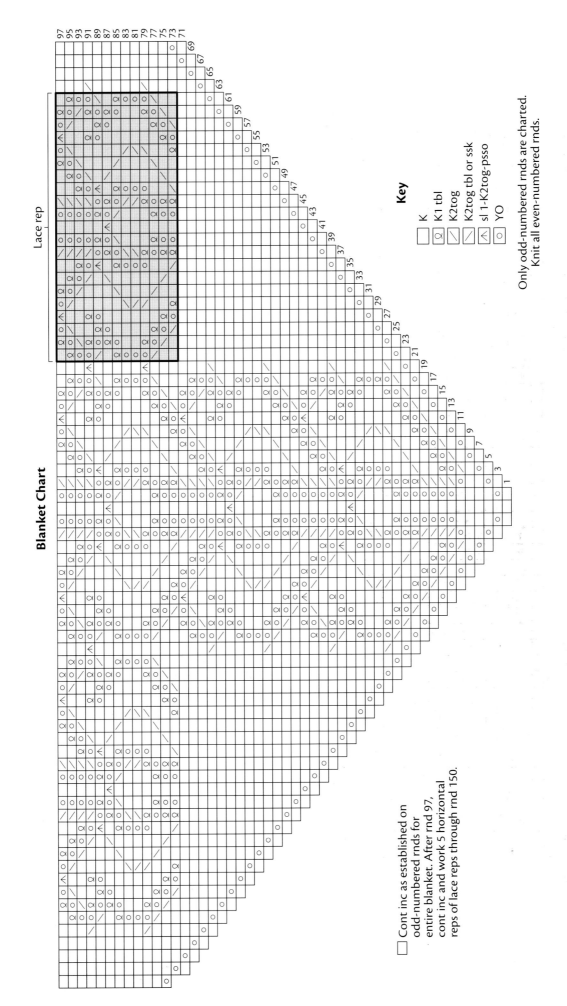

**Blanket Chart**

Lace rep

**Key**

| | K |
| α | K1 tbl |
| / | K2tog |
| \ | K2tog tbl or ssk |
| ⟨ | sl 1-K2tog-psso |
| ○ | YO |

Only odd-numbered rnds are charted.
Knit all even-numbered rnds.

☐ Cont inc as established on
odd-numbered rnds for
entire blanket. After rnd 97,
cont inc and work 5 horizontal
reps of lace reps through rnd 150.

# Kitty Cat Raglan PULLOVER
## *Designed by Jean Scorgie*

These kitties face toward each side of this sweater,
just like the designer's kitty Clipper who loves to tuck his head
into the crook of her arm when he sits on her lap. Because this
yarn is somewhat slippery, Jean found it much easier to
knit on bamboo needles rather than metal ones.

**Skill Level:** Intermediate ◗■■▭

**Size:** S (M, L)

**Finished Bust:** 38 (42, 45)"

**Finished Length:** 24½ (26½, 28½)"

## MATERIALS

9 (11, 12) skeins of Suri Merino from Plymouth Yarn Company (55% suri alpaca, 45% extra fine merino wool; 50 g; 110 yds) in color 5297 Peacock Blue

Size 6 (4 mm) circular needle, 29" long, or size to obtain gauge

Size 5 (3.75 mm) circular needle, 29" long

2 spare circular needles to hold set-aside stitches

8 stitch holders or waste yarn

6 stitch markers

1 safety pin

Tapestry needle

**Gauge:** 18 sts and 28 rows = 4" in St st on larger needle

## FRONT

With larger needle, CO 86 (94, 102) sts. Change to smaller needle and work 4 rows of rev St st. Change to larger needle and work 8 rows of St st.

**Next row (RS):** K12 (13, 17), pm, work row 1 of left-facing kitty chart (page 107) over 28 sts, pm, K6 (12, 12), pm, work row 1 of right-facing kitty chart (page 107) over 28 sts, pm, K12 (13, 17).

**Next row (WS):** Purl.

Cont patt as established until kitties are complete.

Cont in St st until piece measures 15 (16, 17)" or desired length to underarm. End after a RS row. Place sts on a spare circular needle and transfer first and last 6 (7, 8) sts for underarm onto small st holders or waste yarn—74 (80, 86) sts rem in front. Set aside.

## BACK

With larger needle, CO 87 (95, 103) sts.

Change to smaller needle and work 4 rows of rev St st.

Change to larger needle and work in St st until piece measures 15 (16, 17)" or same as front. End after a RS row. Place sts on a second spare circular needle and transfer first and last 6 (7, 8) sts for underarm onto small st holders or waste yarn—75 (81, 87) sts rem in back. Set aside.

## SLEEVES

With larger needle, CO 43 (47, 51) sts for first sleeve.

Change to smaller needle and work 4 rows of rev St st. Change to larger needle, work in St st and AT SAME TIME, inc 1 st at each end of a RS row every 4 rows 18 times—79 (83, 87) sts per sleeve. End after a WS row.

Next row (RS): K33 (35, 37), pm, work row 1 of kitty head chart (page 107) for 13 sts, pm, K33 (35, 37).

Next row (WS): Purl.

Cont as established until kitty face is complete.

Cont in St st until total length measures 16 (17, 18)" or desired length. End after a RS row.

Place sts on spare circular needle next to back sts and transfer first and last 6 (7, 8) sts to holders or waste yarn—67 (69, 71) sts.

Rep for second sleeve and place sts on other side of back sts.

## JOIN BODY AND SLEEVES FOR YOKE

With larger needle, work across first 37 (40, 43) sts of front, pm, work to end of front, work across 67 (69, 71) sts of first sleeve, work across 75 (81, 87) sts of back, work across 67 (69, 71) sts of second sleeve—283 (299, 315) total sts in yoke. Work across to first marker (center front).

Next row: Turn. Purl around to center front marker.

## SHAPE RAGLAN AND V-NECK

Row 1: K2, K2tog, *knit to 3 sts before raglan marker, work dec as follows: K2tog tbl, K1, sm, K1, K2tog, rep, from * 3 times, knit to 4 sts from end, K2tog tbl, K2.

Row 2: Purl.

Rep these 2 rows 11 (12, 13) times. Then stop V-neck decs but cont raglan decs. AT SAME TIME, work a kitty face on back as follows:

Next row (RS): PM 13 sts apart in center of back and work row 1 of kitty face chart.

Next row (WS): Purl.

Cont as established until kitty face is complete. Cont working raglan decs until there are 3 sts on each front before markers.

Next row (RS): K1, K2tog, sm, K1, K2tog, knit across sleeve, work raglan decs, knit across back, work raglan decs, knit across other sleeve, K2tog tbl, K1, sm, K2tog tbl, K1.

Next row: Purl.

Next row: *BO 6, work around, cont raglan decs.

Next row: BO 6 and purl rem sts.

Rep from * once.

Next row: BO rem sts, leaving the last loop on needle to beg neckline finish.

## V-NECK EDGE

To avoid stretching the neckline, work alternate rows of the neckline finish with the smaller and larger needles. On the second row after picking up the neckline sts, turn the work so that you are knitting on WS (rev St st) rather than purling on RS.

Place the loop on the smaller needle, and with RS facing, PU 1 st for each st or dec row at the center front, but on the straight sides of the front neckline, pick up 2 sts every 3 rows. With larger needle, knit 1 rnd with RS facing. Turn work so WS is facing you, and with larger needle, knit 1 rnd. Cont knitting another rnd with the larger needle, and a third rnd with smaller needle. On the next rnd with the larger needle, BO all sts loosely.

## FINISHING

Sew side and underarm seams. Join the underarm sleeve sts to the matching body sts with Kitchener st (see page 110). Work in all loose yarn tails. Steam press lightly.

## Left-Facing Kitty (Peruvian Cat)

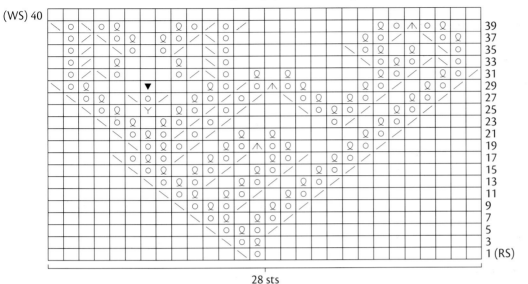

28 sts

## Right-Facing Kitty (Peruvian Cat)

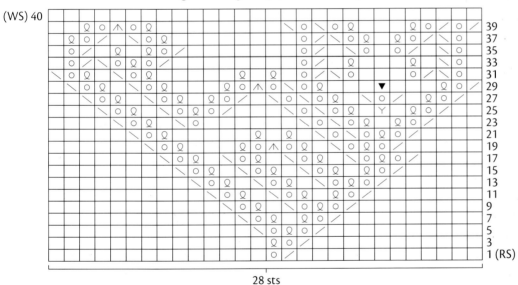

28 sts

## Kitty Head (Peruvian Cat Head)

13 sts

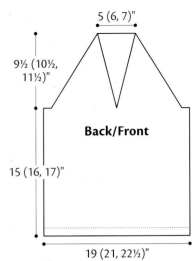

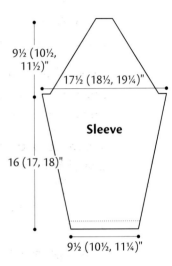

### Key

| | |
|---|---|
| ☐ K on RS, P on WS | ⋀ sl 1-K2tog-psso |
| Ⓠ K1 tbl | ○ YO |
| ╱ K2tog | Y K1 f&b |
| ╲ K2tog tbl or ssk | ▼ K st through open space below |

Only odd-numbered rows are charted.
Purl all even-numbered rows.

# Abbreviations

| | |
|---|---|
| approx | approximately |
| beg | begin(ning) |
| BO | bind off |
| CC | contrasting color |
| ch | chain |
| CO | cast on |
| cont | continue(ing)(s) |
| cw | conceal wrap (see "Short Rows" on page 110) |
| dec | decrease(ing)(s) |
| dpn(s) | double-pointed needle(s) |
| EOR | every other row |
| g | gram(s) |
| inc(s) | increase(ing)(s) |
| K | knit |
| K1f&b | knit into front and back of same stitch—1 stitch increased |
| K1 tbl | knit 1 stitch through the back loop |
| K2tog | knit 2 stitches together; a right-slanting decrease—1 stitch decreased |
| K2tog tbl | knit 2 stitches together through the back loops; a left-slanting decrease—1 stitch decreased |
| K3tog | knit 3 stitches together—2 stitches decreased |
| kw | knitwise, as if to knit |
| LLinc | Insert left needle, from back to front, into st 2 rnds below the st just knit; place onto left needle and knit through back loop. |
| LRinc | Insert right needle, from back to front, into st below the next st to be knit; place on left needle and knit. |
| m | meter(s) |

| | |
|---|---|
| M1 | make 1 stitch; pick up the horizontal strand of yarn lying between the stitch just worked and the next stitch on the left-hand needle and knit into the back of it—1 stitch increased |
| MC | main color |
| mm | millimeter(s) |
| oz | ounce(s) |
| P | purl |
| P2tog | purl 2 stitches together—1 stitch decreased |
| P3tog | purl 3 stitches together—2 stitches decreased |
| patt | pattern(s) |
| pm | place marker |
| prev | previous |
| psso | pass slipped stitch over |
| PU | pick up and knit |
| pw | purlwise, as if to purl |
| rem | remain(ing)(s) |
| rep(s) | repeat(s) |
| rev St st | reverse stockinette stitch: purl on right side, knit on wrong side |
| rnd(s) | round(s) |
| RS | right side |
| sl | slip |
| sl1-K1-psso | slip 1 stitch knitwise, knit 1 stitch, pass slipped stitch over; a left-slanting decrease—1 stitch decreased |
| sl1-K2tog-psso | slip 1 stitch knitwise, knit 2 together, pass slipped stitch over the knit 2 together; a left-slanting decrease—2 stitches decreased |

sl2-K1-p2sso
  slip 2 stitches knitwise, knit 1, pass 2 slipped stitches over—2 stitches decreased

sm  slip marker

ssk  slip 2 stitches, 1 at a time, as if to knit, then insert left needle from left to right into front loops and knit 2 stitches together; a left-slanting decrease—1 stitch decreased

ssp  slip 2 stitches, 1 at a time, as if to knit. Transfer stitches back to the left needle. Insert the right needle from left to right through the back of the stitches and purl the two together from that position; a left-slanting decrease—1 stitch decreased

sssk  slip, slip, slip, knit 3 stitches together—2 stitches decreased

st(s)  stitch(es)

St st(s)  stockinette stitch(es): back and forth—knit on right side, purl on wrong side; in the round—knit every round

tbl  through back loop(s)

tog  together

w&t  wrap and turn (see "Short Rows" on page 110)

WS  wrong side

wyib  with yarn in back

wyif  with yarn in front

yd(s)  yard(s)

YO(s)  yarn over(s)

# Resources

Refer to the websites of the following companies to find retail shops that carry yarns featured in this book.

**Artyarns**
www.artyarns.com
Silk Rhapsody and Silk Mohair

**Brown Sheep Company**
www.brownsheep.com
Burly Spun, Cotton Fleece, and Lamb's Pride Superwash Worsted

**Cherry Tree Hill Yarn**
www.cherryyarn.com
Silky Kidd, Supersock DK, and Supersock Select Semisolids

**JaggerSpun**
www.jaggeryarn.com
Maine Line 2/8

**Lorna's Laces**
www.lornaslaces.net
Lion & Lamb, Shepherd Sock, Shepherd Sport, Swirl Chunky, and Swirl DK

**Louet**
www.louet.com
Gems Merino

**Plymouth Yarn Company**
www.plymouthyarn.com
Bristol Yarn Gallery Buckingham and Suri Merino

**Schoolhouse Press**
www.schoolhousepress.com
Jamieson & Smith Shetland Lace-weight and Jumper-weight Yarns

**Skacel**
www.skacelknitting.com
Zitron Trekking Pro Natura Sock Yarn

**Yarn Place**
www.yarnplace.com
Adagio Fingering

# Glossary

## SEED STITCH

**Flat:** Worked over an odd number of sts.

**Circular:** Worked over an even number of sts.

**Row/rnd 1 (RS):** *K1, P1; rep from *; for flat knitting only, knit last st of row.

**Row/rnd 2:** Knit the purl sts and purl the knit sts as they face you.

Rep row/rnd 2 for patt.

## SHORT ROWS

Short rows are used for shaping garments and accessories by knitting only a part of the row. The yarn must be wrapped around the turning stitch to avoid having holes in the work.

### Wrap and Turn (w&t)

**On a knit row:** Sl the next st, bring yarn forward, sl st back to left needle, bring yarn back; turn and work following row as instructed.

**On a purl row:** Sl the next st, bring yarn back, sl st back to left needle, bring yarn forward; turn and work following row as instructed.

Note that there are several ways to work a w&t. If you work the wraps in a different way, that's fine. Use the technique that is comfortable to you.

### Pick Up and Work Wrap(s)

When you work back across the row where you made a w&t, you need to hide the wrap.

**Conceal wrap (cw):** Insert the needle into yarn wrapped around the next st (in some cases, there may be more than one wrap). Place the wrap(s) on the needle next to its st. Knit or purl (as appropriate) both the wrap(s) and st as a single st.

Sometimes you will be hiding a wrap and working a decrease at the same time:

**cw/ssk:** Conceal wrap while also dec 1 st by including the following st in the ssk portion of the cw such that you are knitting the 2 sts and the wrap together as if you were performing an sssk.

**cw/P2tog:** Conceal wrap while also dec 1 st by including the following st in the P2tog portion of the cw such that you are purling 2 sts and the wrap tog as if performing a P3tog.

## KITCHENER STITCH (OR GRAFTING)

Arrange sts to be joined, so that top of foot sts are on one needle, and rem sts on another needle. With sts to be joined on the 2 separate needles, hold needles parallel in same hand so that one needle is in front of the other with needle points to the right, and yarn end is coming off to the right. As you work, bring yarn under needles when moving between needles. Adjust tension of sewn sts as necessary to match knitted fabric.

Begin by "sewing" with tapestry needle into first st on front needle as if to purl; then "sew" into first st on back needle as if to knit.

Rep the following 4 steps until only the last st rem on each of the front and back needles:

On front needle:

1. "Sew" into first st as to knit, sl this st off needle.

2. "Sew" into second st as to purl.

On back needle:

3. "Sew" into first st as to purl, sl this st off needle.

4. "Sew" into second st as to knit.

End by working steps 1 and 3 only. Bring yarn end through to inside of garment.

# Designer Bios

**Evelyn A. Clark** is a Pacific Northwest native who left a corporate career for a simpler life, and then discovered a passion for lace knitting and spinning. Evelyn won the first buffalo fiber contest held by *Wild Fibers* magazine, and her book *Knitting Lace Triangles* was published by Fiber Trends in 2007. Visit her at www.evelynclarkdesigns.com.

**Ava Coleman** began marketing her own knits at age 16. Since then, she has designed and knit for numerous companies and also writes articles about knitting history. Chosen as a Colorado State Heritage Artist in 1997, her knitted lace designs have been showcased in museums and galleries, including Denver International Airport's Public Art Gallery.

**Sauniell Nicole Connally** took up knitting in 2001, and two years later she was designing garment patterns for herself and for publication on her website, saunshine.blogspot.com. Propelled by her love of knitwear and her lifelong passion for fashion design, she is honing her skills at the Fashion Institute of Technology in New York.

**L'Tanya Durante** has been knitting and crocheting since she was a teenager. As the publisher and editor of *Black Purl* magazine and the author of the blog Craftnicity, she has the wonderful opportunity to incorporate her love for all things crafty, cultural, historical, and ethnic.

**Jackie Erickson-Schweitzer** (Jackie E-S) is a longtime knitting enthusiast who shares her experience through designing, publishing, and teaching. She enjoys the intriguing possibilities of hand-knitted lace—harmonizing the lacy light and shadow with the style and function of the intended article. Her HeartStrings patterns are available at many retailers and can be seen at www.heartstringsfiberarts.com.

**Chrissy Gardiner**, a former software architect, dabbled in fiber arts for years, but knitting became an obsession after her kids were born and she left the corporate world. She is the founder of Gardiner Yarn Works and a regular contributor to *Interweave Knits* magazine. She also teaches knitting at shops around Portland, Oregon.

**Renee Leverington** lives in Iowa, but spent much of her Arizona childhood working on crochet projects. She taught herself to knit 20 years ago by making a pair of gloves for her mom—the stitches were a bit tight but they fit! Her line of knitwear patterns, "Goddess Knits," includes shawls and socks. Renee is married and has a daughter, a grandson, and three "fur kids."

**Karin Maag-Tanchak** grew up in Germany and learned knitting as a child. She almost never used written patterns until she opened a yarn shop and had to sell patterns to her customers. She has been published in *No Sheep for You* and *Knit 'N Style* magazine, written patterns for Decadent Fibers, and maintains her blog www.knitting-and.blogspot.com.

**Marnie MacLean** began designing her own knits around 2003, and although she's produced some spectacular knitting tragedies, she likes to think they've led to a greater appreciation of the way yarn and technique can come together. For a multitude of patterns plus Marnie's thoughts on knitting, crocheting, spinning, and dogs, visit www.marniemaclean.com.

**Annie Modesitt** lives in St. Paul where she designs, writes, and raises her redheaded kids. A self-taught knitter, for years she felt "wrong but happy" with her intuitive yet peculiar style, until she came upon the term "combination knitting" and finally felt legitimate. She teaches around the world and loves interacting with knitters of all ages and cultures.

**Debbie O'Neill** is a software engineer but spends her free time teaching knitting and writing patterns. She has done sock designs for TheKnitter.com, the Loopy Ewe, and Cherry Tree Hill Yarn, and she has published her own line of patterns under the name Nutty Creations. Debbie loves to spend time with her family, cook, read, and dabble in other fiber pursuits.

**Cheryl Potter** is a colorist who owns a hand-painted yarn company called Cherry Tree Hill Yarn in Barton, Vermont. She has taught countless classes on color theory and is the author of six knitting books. Besides knitting, coming up with new colorways and new ways to dye yarn is her favorite thing to do.

**Deborah Robson** has been working with textiles since before she could read. She spins, weaves, knits, crochets, and is endlessly intrigued by the many things you can do with fiber. She is the editor, designer, and publisher of Nomad Press, which is dedicated to giving contemporary knitters access to the skills and design techniques of traditional and ethnic knitting and spinning.

**Alice Scherp** was born in Nome, Alaska, in 1941. Her mom worked with the Oomingmak Musk Ox Producers' Co-operative, both as a knitter and as one who "made corrections" in knit items that contained mistakes! Alice joined the Eugene Spinners Guild in 1975, and there she met Dorothy Reade, who taught her how to knit lace. She has been in love with spinning and lace knitting ever since. Alice also does fur and leather sewing, beadwork, and dyeing.

**Kristi Schueler** is a freelance artist and designer. She lives and knits in the home she shares with her husband, Drew, and their rescue dog, Emma, in the foothills of the Colorado Rockies. She loves knitting lace accents in her socks and garments. You can follow her adventures at blog.designedlykristi.com.

**Jean Scorgie**, better known as a hand weaver, learned to knit as a child watching her mother and grandmother knit mittens and sweaters. While teaching weaving at Oregon State University in Corvallis, Oregon, in the early 1970s, she met Dorothy Reade and installed an impressive exhibition of Dorothy's wedding-ring shawls. Jean continued to weave and knit, later becoming editor of *Handwoven* magazine. In 2000, she launched her own publication, *Weaver's Craft*, for beginning and intermediate hand weavers on four- to eight-shaft looms.

# Index